Orders: Please contact www.How2Become.com

You can order through Amazon.co.uk under ISBN 978-1-912370-83-2 via the website www.How2Become.com, or via Gardners.

ISBN: 978-1-912370-83-2

First published in 2020

Typeset by Gemma Butler.

To
Jay, May and Miya.

Note to Parents.

The principal focus of this book is to ensure that pupils in Key Stage Two develop their understanding of Number Skills within Mathematics.

The book is aimed at pupils aged from seven up to twelve years of age studying Key Stage Two, in particular reluctant mathematicians and pupils who struggled in Key Stage One.

The nature of this book means that it will appeal to pupils who are disinterested in straightforward Maths text books. It is designed to deal with mathematical topics, and it can be supplemented with extra input to these topics from you.

The aim of the book is to develop the connections that pupils make between the nature of Number Skills, including addition, subtraction, multiplication and division, incorporating fractions, decimals, percentages and a variety of number patterns, in line with the current national Mathematics curriculum.

The book is designed to enable pupils to develop their ability to solve mathematical problems by providing building blocks for learning in an accessible way.

Michael Wood

CONTENTS

TOPIC   PAGE

More Contents

TOPIC	PAGE

If you bought this book because you think it's all about **CATS**... you'll be disappointed!!

There's only [one] cat in this book, and she's :**NEVER**: around when there's any **maths** on the page...!!

Here's my cat **maisie** ➡

But this is **NOT** how you would normally **SEE** her...

It's more likely that you would see her **LIKE THIS!**

She has the right idea! She *hates* maths!
And I feel {exactly} the same!
Especially when I have a
{ maths test } in school!

It all started when I got the results of
my latest MATHS TEST.
Mr Campbell gave out everybody else's exercise
books, and then, {finally,} he came to {my} desk...

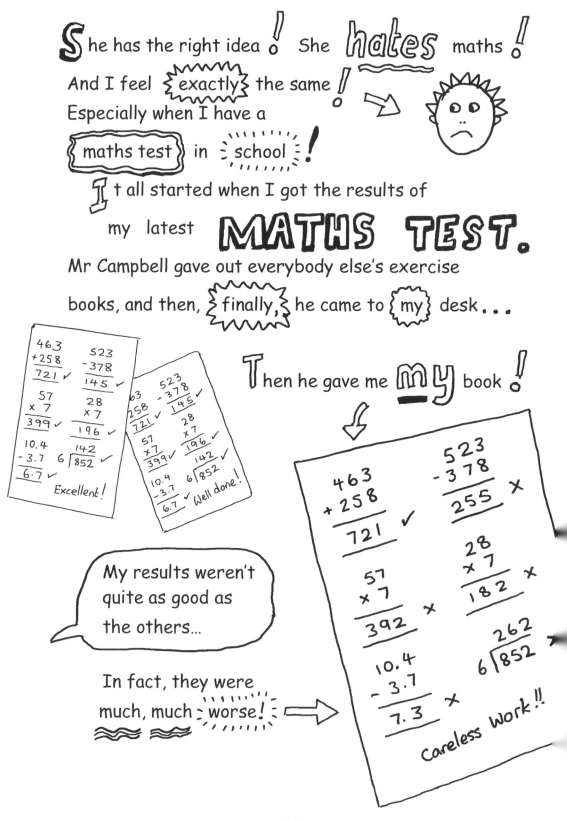

Then he gave me my book!

463
+258
721 ✓

523
-378
145 ✓

57
× 7
399 ✓

28
× 7
196 ✓

10.4
- 3.7
6.7 ✓

142
6⟌852 ✓

Excellent!

523
-378
145 ✓

63
258 ✓
721

28
× 7
196 ✓

57
× 7
399 ✓

142
6⟌852 ✓

10.4
-3.7
6.7 ✓ Well done!

My results weren't
quite as good as
the others...

In fact, they were
much, much worse!

463
+258
721 ✓

523
-378
255 ✗

57
× 7
392 ✗

28
× 7
182 ✗

10.4
- 3.7
7.3 ✗

262
6⟌852

Careless work!!

He must have done it for a [reason] because he glared right at me as he placed my book on my desk, open on the page where all my mistakes were... And he was scowling at me...!

My heart dropped! Two out of ten! TWO? Just two...? That can't be right..! Mr Campbell must have made some mistakes! Maybe he just can't add up! And he had written (in red ink)...

CARELESS WORK! And there were TWO exclamation marks at the end as well...!

Ok! So it's happened! I've had a bit of an OFF DAY! It happens to everybody!? As long as MUM doesn't find out..!

But how can I hide the { evidence } from her ?

Perhaps I should tear out the page in my maths book !

(Maybe not...!)

I've managed to ~ hide ~ the last couple of tests

from her, so can I do it again !?? (hopefully!)

But... **T**hings don't always work out the way you

want them to...!

The moment I enter the house – the ⓔⓧⓐⓒⓣ

moment – { MUM } asks me the question I'm dreading..!

How did you get on with your maths test today, Jack?

Oh. Err.... Ok. . .

Act casual...! Just sound smooth!

Well? Show me your test!

Ok. Stay casual. Keep cool...

Oh... Err... I left it at school...!

Jack! I always know when you're not telling the truth! Show me your book!!

Well, I suppose there's no way around it.. As usual, Mum knows what's what. I 'm well and truly caught...

... like a wriggling fish on a fishing line...

Very slowly, I pull my maths book out of my bag.

Two! Two out of ten! That's very poor!

Maisie knows what's coming next. She just runs off in disgust! (I wish I could...!)

I revert to my next tactic. Everything is carefully planned ... !

It was one of the highest marks in the class...
It was a very **difficult** test... !

maybe I'm being a bit optimistic here

You **HAVE** to believe me !

The look on Mum's face told me that she probably wasn't going to believe me ! I was officially →→→→→ IN TROUBLE ... !

I was going to explain that I did actually get **TWO** answers perfectly correct... ! ⇨ ✓✓

... But I suppose the reply would have been that I still had EIGHT wrong . ⇨ ✗ ✗ ✗ ✗ ✗ ✗ ✗ ✗

I am going to get a ⸰tutor⸰ to help you with your maths work... !

No! Not necessary! You don't have to bother!

Panic was starting to set in...

And that's how I end up getting officially

T U T O R E D.

My reaction when I'm told!

To tell you the truth, the idea of a tutor turned out far worse than what actually happened ...

What put me off was the thought of all that **EXTRA** maths for a whole hour every week!

But... it wasn't that **bad**. In fact, if I was honest, I learned quite a lot And the hour went past very quickly!

Well, his name is Mr Prentice and I remember that clearly, because his first joke is...

I'm Mr Prentice, and you're my APprentice!

Ok. So it's not a good joke, and I realise quickly that he has LOTS and LOTS of UN funny jokes! In fact, some of them are very BAD...!

So, what did I actually learn?

In the first lesson, I learn about  PLACE VALUE.

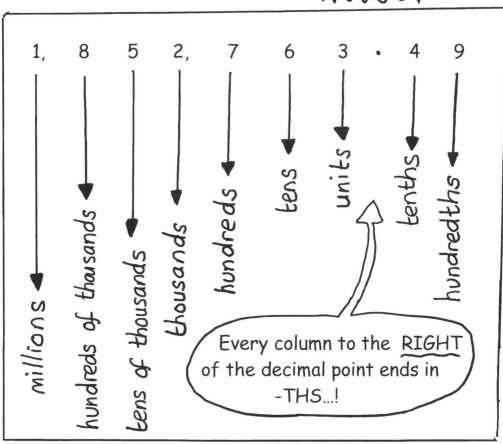

1,   8   5   2,   7   6   3   •   4   9

millions
hundreds of thousands
tens of thousands
thousands
hundreds
tens
units
tenths
hundredths

Every column to the RIGHT of the decimal point ends in -THS...!

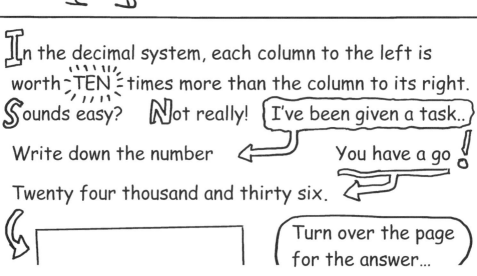

In the decimal system, each column to the left is worth TEN times more than the column to its right. Sounds easy? Not really! I've been given a task..

Write down the number

You have a go!

Twenty four thousand and thirty six.

Turn over the page for the answer...

18

→ {24,036} ←

D id you get it right? **B** ecause I didn't... !

So he's given me a few more to do...

W rite down these numbers in figures

1. Twelve thousand and sixteen

2. Fifteen thousand one hundred

3. Thirty-five thousand and fifteen

4. Nine thousand and nine

5. In the number 1,584, how many does the 5 represent?

6. In the number 42,508, how many does the 4 represent?

7. In the number 4,719, how many does the nine represent?

W ell, I got nearly all of those right this time !

(They're not easy!) (**A** nswers on page 137..)

Well, I'm not sure about Mr Prentice YET, but at least I'm learning some Maths!

Now I've got some more work to do on place order.

Here's some Jumbled numbers.

(45) (72) (50) (44) (71) (39)

1. Write these numbers in order, from the smallest to the biggest!

☐ ☐ ☐ ☐ ☐ ☐

Here's some more numbers, but this time they have different amounts of digits, so that makes it a bit more difficult!

2. Put these in order, from smallest to biggest.

(463) (78) (12,032) (984) (69) (4,207)

☐ ☐ ☐ ☐ ☐ ☐

Jumbled brain!

Answers on page 137

Those weren't too bad! I think I got them right!

... But now there's even more work to do...

Look at these numbers.

(5)   (2)   (1)   (7)   (8)

1. Write down the { biggest number } you can make

using ALL the numbers above. [   ]

2. Write down the { smallest number } you can make

using ALL the numbers above. [   ]

Now write these { numbers } in words.

3. 3 0 6 [   ]

4. 4,0 1 2 [   ]

5. 2 0 6,0 5 0 [   ]

[   ]

Answers on
page 137...

That last one is tough !

And I think my tutor forgets that I'm

allergic to writing ! ⟹

Sometimes you get problems like this.

Write as a number (15 tens) and (12 units)

15 doesn't fit into the tens column, so it over-flows into the hundreds column.

12 doesn't fit into the units column, so it overflows into the tens column.

So 15 tens is the same as 1 in the hundreds column and 5 in the tens column.

And 12 units is the same as 1 in the tens column and 2 in the units column.

So the answer is ⇨

$$
\begin{array}{r}
1\ 5\ 0 \\
1\ 2\ + \\
\hline
1\ 6\ 2
\end{array}
$$

Answers on Page 137

Now have a go at these. Write each as a number.

1. 14 tens and 17 units

2. 16 hundreds and 13 tens

3. 25 tens and 25 units

I think Mr P makes things difficult on purpose...!

The next topic is ADDITION! ⊕
+ + + + + + + + +

(Even though I think I know everything about it!)

When you are adding up a long string of numbers, there's things you can do to make it easier...!

Look at : –

4 + 2 + 6 + 8 + 5 + 9 + 7 + 5 + 3...

Adding all that lot up involves lots of fingers!

But there's an easier way to do it.

Link up all the numbers that add up to TEN...

4 + 2 + 6 + 8 + 5 + 9 + 7 + 5 + 3

So, there's 4 lots of 10, plus the left-over 9 = 49

4 9
2 7
8 1
6 3

+

It also works with LARGER numbers!

Maisie is not impressed...

She only cares if it
+ + + + + +
+ adds up + to more FOOD!
+ + + + + +

Now add this up!

23

The answer is 〈 2 2 0. 〉 Did you get it right?

(I forgot to carry the 2 into the tens column!)

Subtraction is next on the list!

This time it's all about ... Borrowing,

which I've ˑnever˖ really understood.

But it's not too bad. Here's some 〈 tips! 〉

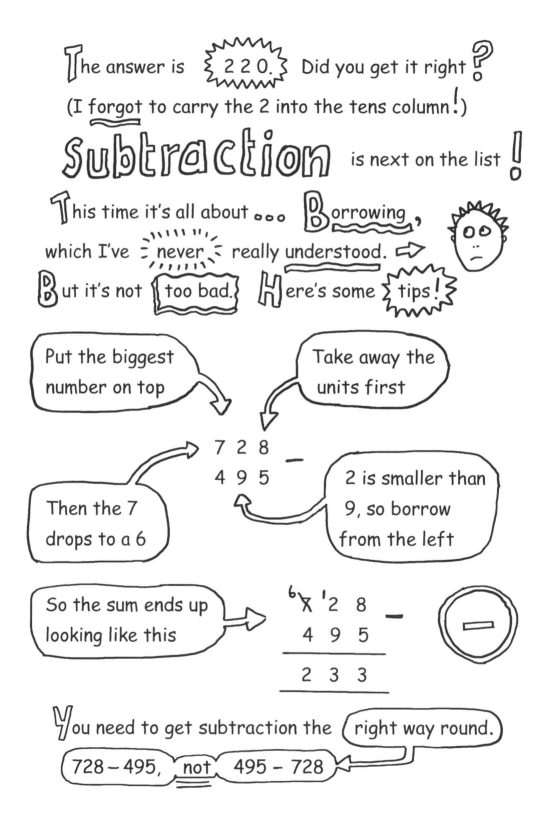

Put the biggest number on top

Take away the units first

```
7 2 8
4 9 5  −
```

Then the 7 drops to a 6

2 is smaller than 9, so borrow from the left

So the sum ends up looking like this

```
 6   1
 7́  ́2  8  −
 4   9  5
─────────
 2   3  3
─────────
```

You need to get subtraction the right way round.

728 − 495, not 495 − 728

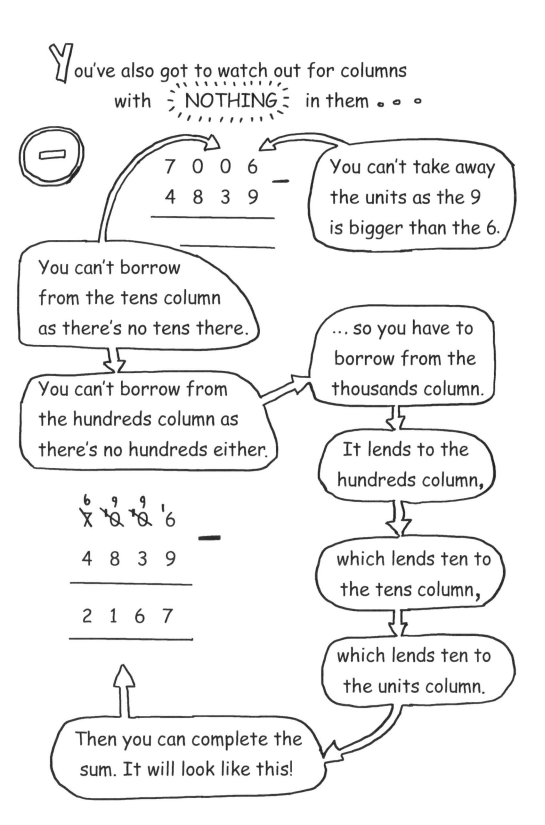

Borrowing is something I mustn't forget!

Mr P rentice says...

> If you borrow someone's giraffe, always remember to give it back!

I think it's his idea of a joke...?
I've already told you he makes lots of very **unfunny** jokes...!

But I think he's getting worse!

I suppose I will have to put up with it for the time being...!
He's useful in some ways.

And my **Maths** skills are *improving!*

But his jokes are definitely a **Pain in the neck!**

> Why was the giraffe so good at maths?

> Because he was head and shoulders above the rest of the class!

Here's the homework I've been set.

(See if you can get them all right !)

```
  3 7 4  _      5 1 8  _      6 0 2  _
  1 2 6         3 8 3         4 7 5
_____      _____      _____


_____      _____      _____
```

```
  5 1 0 4  _    9 0 0 7  _    7 0 0 2  _
  2 9 6 6       1 5 7 9       6 4 3 6
_____    _____    _____


_____    _____    _____
```

He's also given me { these. } Can you finish them ?

```
  4  5 ☐            8 ☐ 4             ☐ 4  8
  2 ☐ 3   +        ☐ 5 ☐    +        3 ☐ 4   +
_____        _____          _____
☐ 9  6             9 9 2             8 7  2
```

Answers on page 137

27

Ok! So my first session with Mr. Prentice wasn't TOO bad...!

(but I do need to think of a nickname for him...!)

And my maths skills are starting to improve! But I mustn't tell MUM...!

The next time I see Prenty he says to me -

Now we're looking at Multiplication!

Oh, no...! I HATE TABLES! I tell him..

He says:

You need to know your tables. but pretend you're playing a GAME !! Once you know your tables, you know them for ever!

And he explains that there's lots of little tricks that you can use to help you learn them! (Which sounds good to me!

Firstly, the **two** times table is: EASY!

If you know [odd] and [even] numbers, you're halfway there! { Every } answer on the T WO times table is...

EVEN!!

So just count up using only EVEN numbers!

They always end in 2, 4, 6, 8 or 0.

3 The **three** times table isn't too bad!

There is a { little trick } you can do, so that you know that a number is on the THREE times table!

Just ADD all the digits (numbers) together!

So, if you add all the digits in 1, 2 7 3 (1 + 2 + 7 + 3), the total comes to... 1 3!

Is 1 3 on the 3 times table? NO. So nor is 1, 2 7 3!

Look at 3 1 4, 1 2 1. The digits add up to 1 2!

Is 1 2 on the 3 times table? YES!

So 3 1 4, 1 2 1 is also on the three times table... !

Easy, eh? I'm starting to get the hang of this maths stuff!

29

4 The FOUR times table isn't bad either.

If you're struggling with 6 × 4, for instance,

think of it as 6 × 2 × 2.

The answers are always [EVEN]!

It can sometimes make it a bit easier...

5 Then there's the FIVE times table!

If FIVE is multiplied by an EVEN number,

the answer always ends in a ZERO!

If FIVE is multiplied by an ODD number,

the answer always ends in a FIVE!

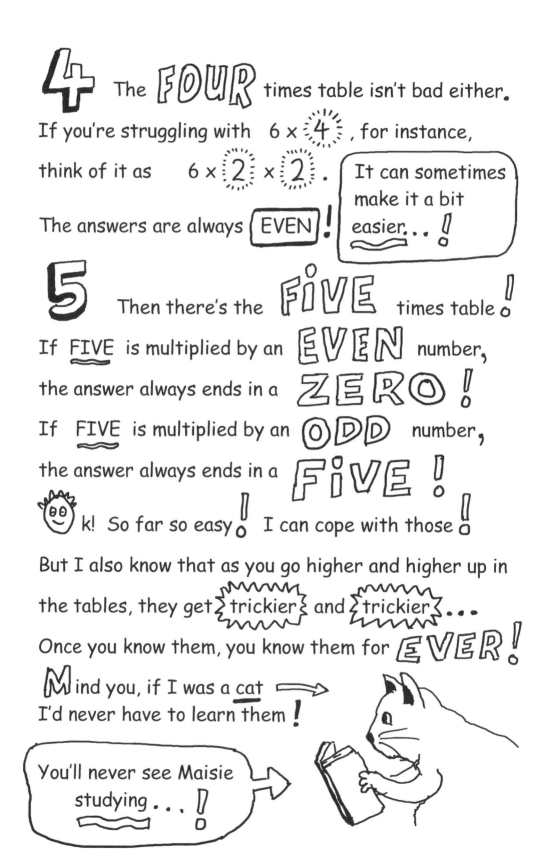

k! So far so easy! I can cope with those!

But I also know that as you go higher and higher up in

the tables, they get trickier and trickier...

Once you know them, you know them for EVER!

Mind you, if I was a cat ⟹
I'd never have to learn them!

You'll never see Maisie studying...!

6 Then there's the SIX times table.

If you're on 8 × 6 for instance,

Think of it as 8 × 2 × 3 !

Multiplying by ⑥ is the same as multiplying by 2, then 3...!

Like we did in the four times table!

7 The SEVEN times table is just tough!

You have to learn it! It has alternate odd and even

numbers:

7	14	21	28	35	42	49	56	63	70

8 When it comes to the EIGHT times table,

it can be easier if you think of 6 × 8 as

6 × 2 × 2 × 2 ! There's other ways too!

With the tables on this page, if you're working out

something higher than 5, you can go back to 5,

and then work your way up to the answer you want.

If you want to work out 8 × 7, go back to ➡ 8 × 5 = 40

(Everybody knows the 5 times tables!)

Then add 8 to it to get ➡ 8 × 6 = 48

Then add another 8 to get ➡ 8 × 7 = 56 !

9 So we come to the NINE times table!

Prento (!!) has told me a way that I will ALWAYS remember the { nine } times tables. And all I need is my [FINGERS.]

Here's how it works!

Hold your hands up, palms facing you...

Imagine that each of your fingers is numbered from 1 to 10, going from left to right!

Now work out what you want the answer to, and then bend that finger down...

So, if you want to find 9 x 6, bend finger number { SIX } down..

(That's the [little finger] on your right hand!)

tens   units

Count all the fingers to the [left] of that finger.
They're the [TENS.] There's *FIVE* of them!
Now count all the fingers to the [right] of that finger
They're the [UNITS.] There's *FOUR* of them!
So the answer is ➔ **54!**

It works with all the 9 times table all the way up to to 9 x 10.

so 9 x 10 has 9 tens and no units = 90

That's the {NINE} times table well and truly sorted!

10 And the **TEN** times table is very easy!

Add a **0** after the number you're multiplying ten by.

The thing I've {learnt} is —
Once you KNOW your times tables, multiplying and dividing gets much *easier!*

BUT you do **HAVE** to **LEARN** them!

11 The ELEVEN times table

is easy too - except at the end!

Whatever I'm multiplying by 11,

I just write out the same number **twice**!

That works all the way up to $11 \times 9 = 99$

After that, I need to know that $11 \times 10 = 110$

$11 \times 11 = 121$ and $11 \times 12 = 132$.

Easy!

12 The TWELVE times table is harder!

One way of working it out is if

I multiply the other number by 10

... and then multiply it by 2!

then add the result together.

So 12×6 looks like this,

... and the answer is 72!

$10 \times 6 = 60$

$2 \times 6 = 12$ +

72

Then I need to know that

$12 \times 11 = 132$ and

$12 \times 12 = 144$

Tables?
I hate tables!

And that's it!

34

Here's a little GAME that might help...!

Match up the {equations} with the {answers} below.

When you find the equation and its answer,

shade both of them in!

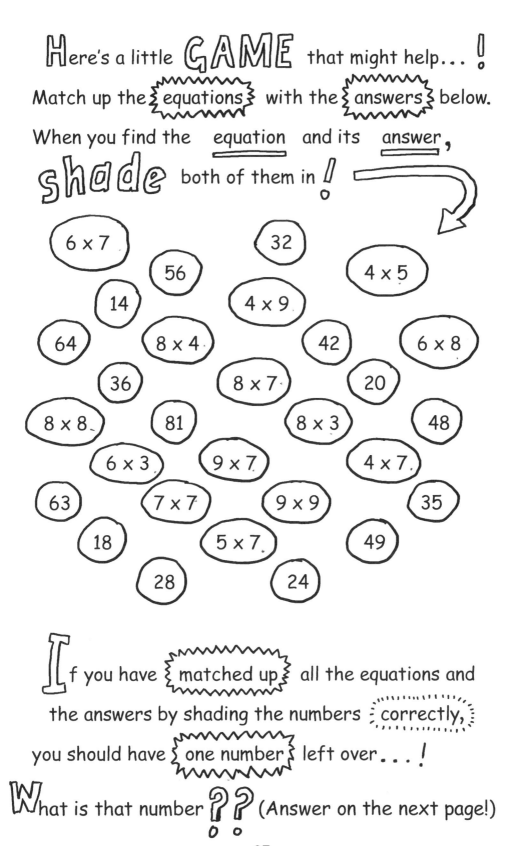

6 x 7 32 4 x 5
56
14 4 x 9
64 8 x 4 42 6 x 8
36 8 x 7 20
8 x 8 81 8 x 3 48
6 x 3 9 x 7 4 x 7
63 7 x 7 9 x 9 35
18 5 x 7 49
28 24

If you have {matched up} all the equations and the answers by shading the numbers correctly, you should have {one number} left over....!

What is that number?? (Answer on the next page!)

The number left over is...

Hard work, but I got that one right!

But, like everything in life, it can get more...

COMPLICATED!

Prento says the opposite of multiplying is dividing
(which I already knew!) So he says that if

$6 \times 7 = 42$ then $42 \div 6 = 7$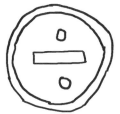

and also $42 \div 7 = 6$

... which makes sense, I suppose!

So, I've decided to give my little brother
a test! (He's only eight, so I didn't
think he'd know the answer...!)

Here is what I asked him:

If $4 \times 6 = 24$, what
is 24 divided by 4 ?

Bob!

(Sadly, he got it right..)

I think **BOB** is a bit of a know-it-all!

But I have a much ~tougher~ test for him!

You need to know your tables going forwards, but

you also need to know them **backwards** too!

Which means you have to know how to ~divide~ them.

So, here's another game:

Match these equations up.

(24 ÷ 3)   (6)   (56 ÷ 8)

  (72 ÷ 8)   (8)

(7)   (30 ÷ 6)   (28 ÷ 7)

   (5)   (9)

(14 ÷ 7)   (27 ÷ 9)   (36 ÷ 6)

   (3)   (48 ÷ 8)   (4)

(6)   (64 ÷ 8)   (2)   (8)

This time there are **NO** numbers left over!

Bob didn't ~stand a chance~ with those!
He's <u>not</u> quite so sure of himself now!

Now **P**rento says we have to look at something called

M U L T I P L E S

He says they're **easy**, but he says that about everything we do..

...and I know that lots of things we do aren't easy!

If a number is a multiple of another number, it means that it appears on that number's times table.

2 For instance, the first eight multiples of are 2, 4, 6, 8, 10, 12, 14, 16, and so on...

(In other words, every **EVEN** number!)

He says that knowing these will help with learning those times tables, which can only help me...!

And he set me this test. Fill in the missing multiples.

Multiples of 3		6			15
Multiples of 7	7				35
Multiples of 8		16		32	

Answers on page 137.

Even BoB filled in some boxes. So I gave him a test...!

1) Look at the numbers in each box below.
Circle the correct multiples of these numbers.

6

| 4 | 24 | 32 | 12 | 34 |
| 28 | 18 | 37 | 36 |

7

| 14 | 37 | 49 | 56 | 25 |
| 30 | 36 | 42 | 27 |

Bob will never get these!

2) How many multiples of 3 are there between 20 and 40?

Here's the answers...!

1) He should have circled 4 multiples in each box!

2) There are 7 multiples of 3

21, 24, 27, 30, 33, 36 and 39.

I was right. Bob didn't get any of them!

Never mind about him...!

I'm certainly feeling more confident about maths now!

At least I can say that I'm not bottom of the class any more!

☐ × ☐ ×
☐ × ☐ ×
☐ × ☐ ×

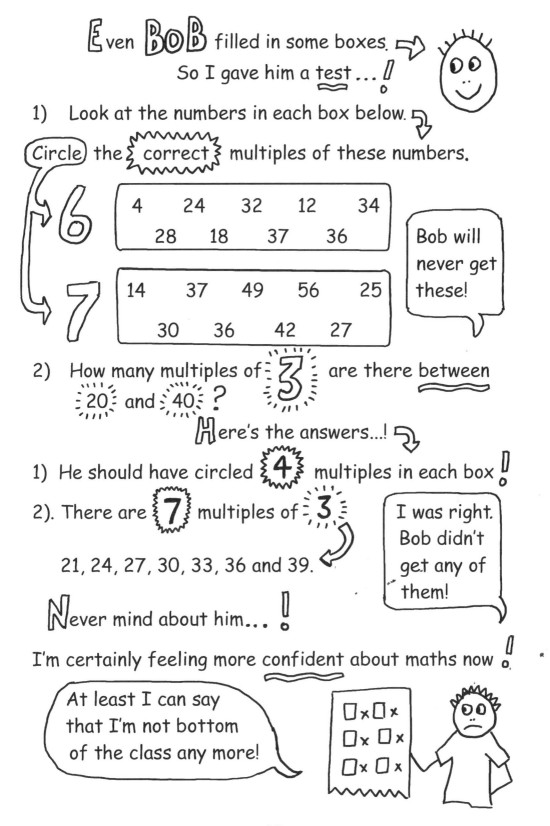

So far, I'm not doing ☼too☼ badly...
(but I'm certainly not going to tell **MUM** yet!)

The next step is ⌇MULTIPLYING SUMS⌇

... which I have been known to get wrong... !

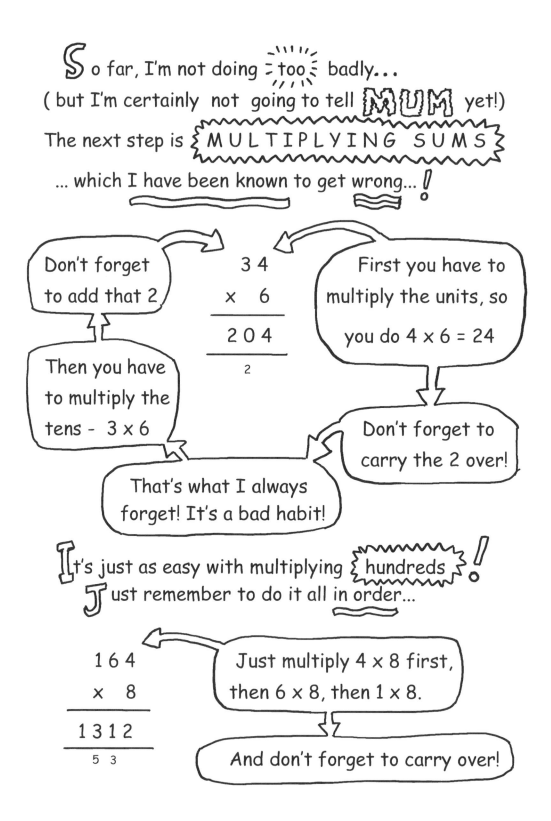

Don't forget
to add that 2

Then you have
to multiply the
tens - 3 x 6

    3 4
  x   6
  —————
    2 0 4
      2

First you have to
multiply the units, so
you do 4 x 6 = 24

Don't forget to
carry the 2 over!

That's what I always
forget! It's a bad habit!

It's just as easy with multiplying ⌇hundreds⌇!
Just remember to do it all in order...

  1 6 4
  x   8
  —————
  1 3 1 2
    5 3

Just multiply 4 x 8 first,
then 6 x 8, then 1 x 8.

And don't forget to carry over!

I know what's coming next! More homework!
(Answers on page 137.)

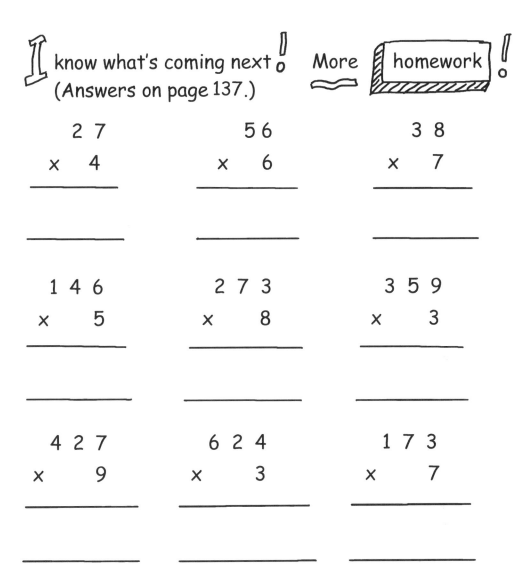

```
    2 7              5 6                  3 8
  x   4            x   6              x    7
  _____        _____          _____

  _____        _____          _____

  1 4 6            2 7 3                3 5 9
  x   5            x   8              x    3
  _____        _____          _____

  _____        _____          _____

  4 2 7            6 2 4                1 7 3
  x   9            x   3              x    7
  _____        _____          _____

  _____        _____          _____
```

So far so good...o I'm ready to move on a bit!
Now Prento says we have to look at ...

 multiplication!
He says it's not too bad, but he's said that before!
So, here goes...

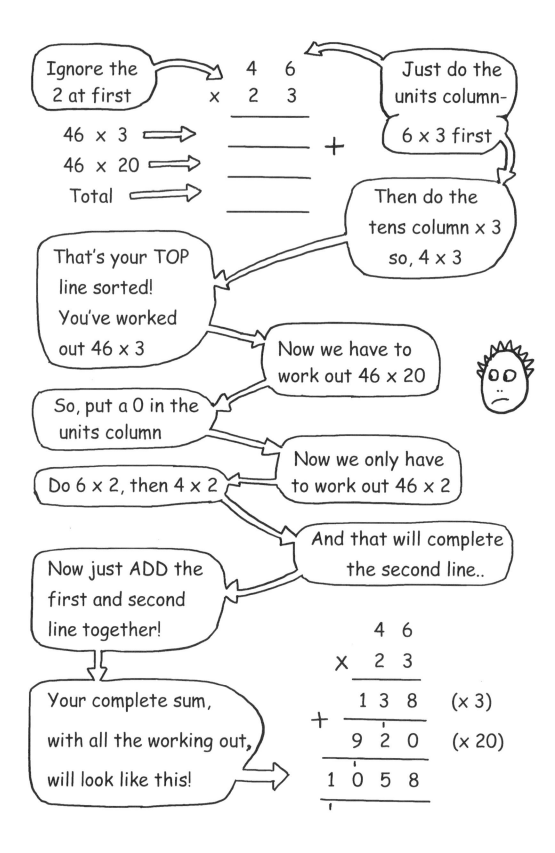

Ignore the 2 at first

4 6
× 2 3

Just do the units column–

6 × 3 first

46 × 3 ⟹
46 × 20 ⟹
Total ⟹

+

Then do the tens column × 3 so, 4 × 3

That's your TOP line sorted! You've worked out 46 × 3

Now we have to work out 46 × 20

So, put a 0 in the units column

Now we only have to work out 46 × 2

Do 6 × 2, then 4 × 2

And that will complete the second line..

Now just ADD the first and second line together!

Your complete sum, with all the working out, will look like this!

4 6
× 2 3

1 3 8   (× 3)
+
9 2 0   (× 20)

1 0 5 8

And that's how **LONG** multiplication works!!

Below the sum, you have to draw in | four | lines

```
        1 3 6
   x      4 7
   _____
```

This line is 136 x 7 →

This line is 136 x 40 →

This is both lines added together! →

That's all there is to it.

Here's a few to try.   (Answers on page 138)

```
      4 5
   x  2 7
   _____

   _____ +
   _____

   _____
```

```
      6 3
   x  3 4
   _____

   _____ +
   _____

   _____
```

```
      2 3
   x  4 5
   _____

   _____ +
   _____

   _____
```

```
   1 3 6
   x 5 2
   _____

   _____ +
   _____

   _____
```

```
   2 4 7
   x  4 3
   _____

   _____ +
   _____

   _____
```

```
   3 2 8
   x  3 6
   _____

   _____ +
   _____

   _____
```

LONG multiplication isn't **EASY!**

You have to remember each part and then do them in the right order!

...and not forget the bits that are carried forward!

There's {two} other things to remember with multiplication. They're **MUCH** simpler!

If you multiply any number by **ZERO**, ...the answer is **ZERO!**

So, 7 6 x 0 = 0, and 3 6 5 x 0 = 0 as well.

That's easy enough!

Also, if any number is multiplied by **ONE**, ...the answer stays **THE SAME!**

So, 7 6 x 1 = 7 6, and 3 6 5 x 1 = 3 6 5!

At least there are a few things in **M**aths that aren't quite so difficult...!

I suppose {multiplication skills} are just part of **EVERYDAY LIFE!**

You'll be pleased to know that **this** page has **NO** long multiplication on it - or {maths} **of any sort.**

Maisie is disgusted with it all!

She has the right idea...

She **hates** Maths!

You can tell because her tail is

bristling...

... and her {whiskers} are twitching !

The only time I see her actually moving is when Mr Prentice appears !

(Then she runs off as quickly as possible!)

Sometimes I wish I could do the same !

But there's no escape for me...

It seems that I'm **STUCK** with Prento

for a **LITTLE WHILE** yet !

Mum is asking me some leading questions.
I have to be careful how I answer them...

How are you getting on with Mr Prentice, Jack?

Err... Ok, I suppose.

I knew that it would help your Maths!

Just play it cool...!

A little bit, maybe. I know nearly all of what we're doing, anyway...

That's great! I thought that seeing him would give you a bit of confidence!

That's typical of her... I never get any credit for anything!

Anyway, Mr **C**lever **C**logs (!) says we need to look at multiplying by (10) and (100) and (1,000) while we are still looking at multiplication.

He says it's all to do with *PLACE VALUE* which we looked at earlier...

So, if you want to multiply any number by 10
you must move all the numbers

ONE place to the $LEFT$!

You have to add a $ZERO$ if it is needed...

Here's where {decimal points} come in.

Look at 47×10. Imagine it as 47.00×10

Move all the digits one place to the left, like this

47.00 becomes 470.0

And that's the answer!

So, here's a few examples:

$164 \times 10 \ = \ 164.0 \times 10 \ = \ 1,640$

$79 \times 10 \ = \ 79.0 \times 10 \ = \ 790$

$3.5 \times 10 \ = \ 35.0 \ = \ 35$

Now here's some for me to do. Answers on page 138

1) $29 \times 10 =$ ☐   2) $75 \times 10 =$ ☐

3) $162 \times 10 =$ ☐   4) $473 \times 10 =$ ☐

5) $6.7 \times 10 =$ ☐   6) $8.5 \times 10 =$ ☐

I got all those right! Easy, aren't they!!

Multiplying by **100** is just as easy!

Just move the numbers **TWO** places to the left

45 x 100 = 45.00 x 100 = 4,500

20 x 100 = 20.00 x 100 = 2,000

23.16 x 100 = 2,316

And... Guess what! When you multiply by **1000** the numbers move **THREE** places to the left.

2.3 x 1,000 = 2.300 x 1,000 = 38,000

Now I have **more** sums to do...!

1) 3.7 x 100 = ☐

2) 7.9 x 100 = ☐

3) 45 x 100 = ☐

4) 61 x 100 = ☐

5) 56 x 1,000 = ☐

6) 9.7 x 1,000 = ☐

7) 2.35 x 1,000 = ☐

8) 45.7 x 1,000 = ☐

I reckon I've got that now! Answers on page 138.

I must admit, I ⟨understood⟩ most of that !

It means I'm ((almost)) looking forward

to my next MATHS test at school, so that I

can show off my new SKILLS !

Perhaps there is a (very small) possibility that

Prenty is actually helping me ... ??

...but I don't want to admit that!

Maths is still a very odd thing to have to do ... !

And I still can't think of a good nickname for him...

Prento?

Pronto?

Prentie?

But there is something about him
that might help me to find a good
NICKNAME !

almost
He's ∧ completely BALD !

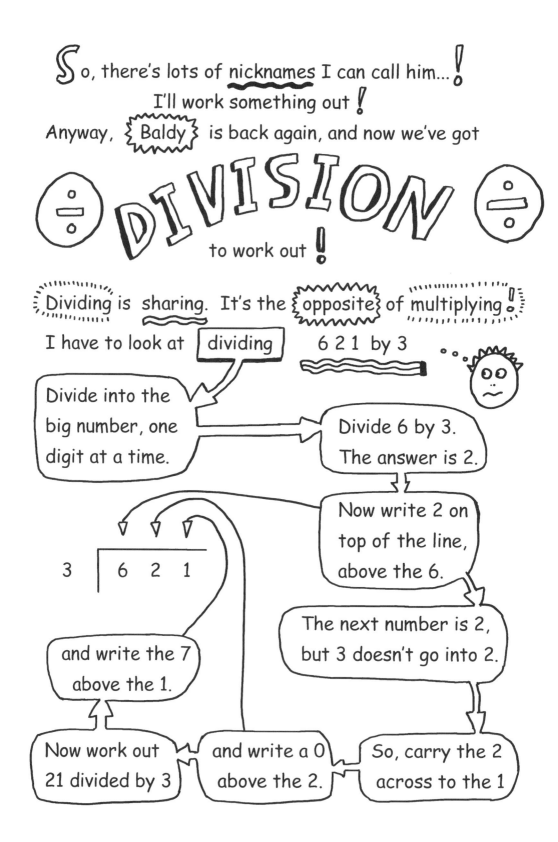

So, there's lots of nicknames I can call him...!
I'll work something out!
Anyway, {Baldy} is back again, and now we've got

DIVISION

to work out!

Dividing is sharing. It's the {opposite} of multiplying!

I have to look at dividing 6 2 1 by 3

Divide into the big number, one digit at a time.

Divide 6 by 3. The answer is 2.

Now write 2 on top of the line, above the 6.

3 | 6 2 1

The next number is 2, but 3 doesn't go into 2.

and write the 7 above the 1.

Now work out 21 divided by 3

and write a 0 above the 2.

So, carry the 2 across to the 1

The completed sum looks like this...!

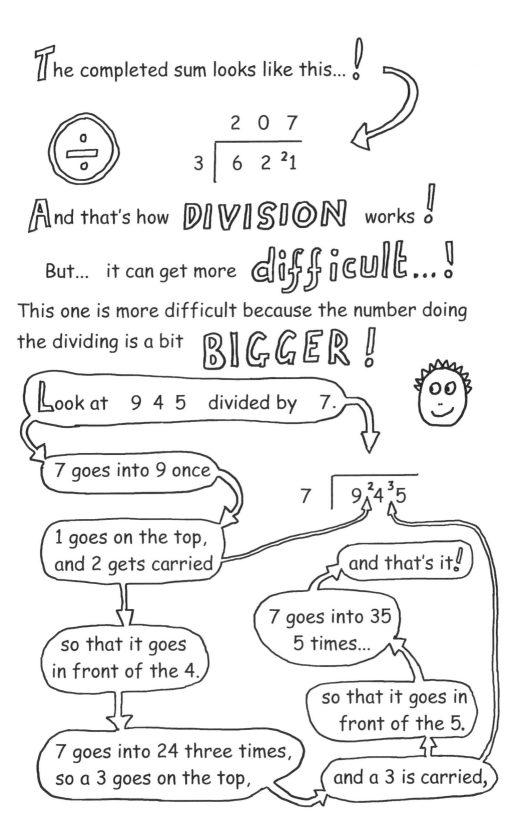

$$\begin{array}{r} 2\ 0\ 7 \\ 3\ \overline{)\ 6\ 2\ ^21\ } \end{array}$$

And that's how **DIVISION** works!

But... it can get more **difficult**...!

This one is more difficult because the number doing

the dividing is a bit **BIGGER!**

Look at 9 4 5 divided by 7.

7 goes into 9 once

1 goes on the top, and 2 gets carried

$$7\ \overline{)\ 9\,^24\,^35\ }$$

and that's it!

so that it goes in front of the 4.

7 goes into 35 5 times...

so that it goes in front of the 5.

7 goes into 24 three times, so a 3 goes on the top,

and a 3 is carried,

So that sum will look like { this } !

I got this one right...! I'm getting better at this !

$$\begin{array}{r} 1\ \ 3\ \ 5 \\ 7\ \overline{)\ 9\ \ ^24\ \ ^35} \end{array}$$

Now ː Baldylocks ˑ has set me { homework } as usual.

Possible new nickname?   I knew he would!

a) $4\ \overline{)\ 6\ \ 1\ \ 2}$ b) $5\ \overline{)\ 8\ \ 2\ \ 5}$

c) $6\ \overline{)\ 7\ \ 4\ \ 4}$ d) $3\ \overline{)\ 8\ \ 8\ \ 8}$

e) $8\ \overline{)\ 9\ \ 8\ \ 4}$ f) $7\ \overline{)\ 8\ \ 7\ \ 5}$

g) $4\ \overline{)\ 9\ \ 5\ \ 6}$ h) $8\ \overline{)\ 9\ \ 5\ \ 2}$

I got most of these right!

Answers on page 138.

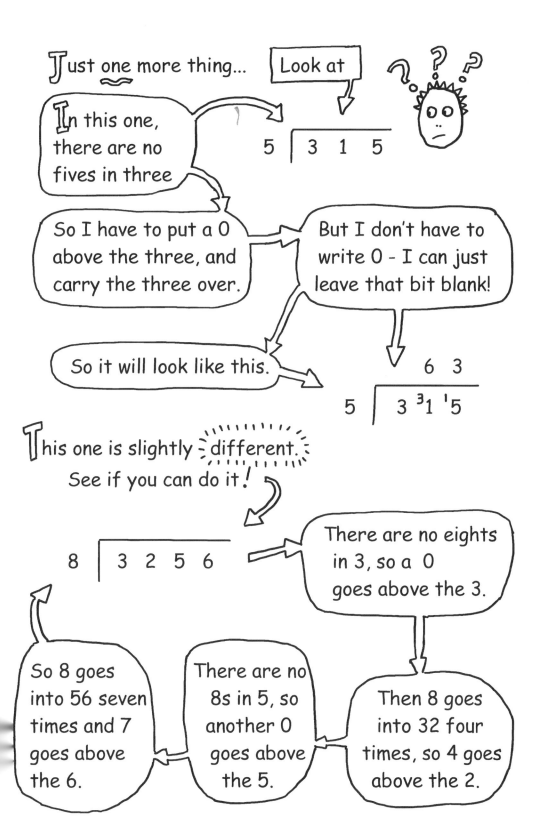

Just one more thing... Look at

In this one, there are no fives in three

$$5 \overline{)\ 3\ \ 1\ \ 5}$$

So I have to put a 0 above the three, and carry the three over.

But I don't have to write 0 - I can just leave that bit blank!

So it will look like this.

$$5 \overline{)\ 3\ {}^3 1\ {}^1 5} \quad 6\ 3$$

This one is slightly different. See if you can do it!

$$8 \overline{)\ 3\ \ 2\ \ 5\ \ 6}$$

There are no eights in 3, so a 0 goes above the 3.

So 8 goes into 56 seven times and 7 goes above the 6.

There are no 8s in 5, so another 0 goes above the 5.

Then 8 goes into 32 four times, so 4 goes above the 2.

Do you remember when I multiplied (The answer to that last sum is 4 0 7.)

by 10, 100 and 1000?

Well, now I have to do the reverse of that...

If I want to DIVIDE any number by 10

I move the numbers ONE place to the RIGHT...

So that means 3 4 0 ÷ 1 0 = 3 4

and 7 8 ÷ 1 0 = 7 . 8

and 2 5 6 ÷ 1 0 = 2 5 . 6

Here you can see that a decimal point has to be added!

It's not so difficult - everything has just moved one space to the right...!

It simply makes the number ten times SMALLER!

Here's a few more that I have to do.

1) 6 7 ÷ 1 0 = ☐

2) 1 8 ÷ 1 0 = ☐

3) 4 5 8 ÷ 1 0 = ☐

4) 3 0 4 ÷ 1 0 = ☐

5) 1 2 3 ÷ 1 0 = ☐

6) 2 ÷ 1 0 = ☐

That last one is tricky, so be extra careful with it.

You just have to take care where to put the

DECIMAL POINT!

Dividing by **100** is fairly straightforward, too!

I move the numbers **TWO** places to the right...

$3\ 6\ 7 \div 1\ 0\ 0 = 3\ .\ 6\ 7$

and $2\ 4 \div 1\ 0\ 0 = 0\ .\ 2\ 4$

I can divide by **1000**
in the same way, so...

> If the number being divided is smaller than the number dividing it, the answer is LESS than one whole!

$1,5\ 8\ 3 \div 1,0\ 0\ 0 = 1\ .5\ 8\ 3$

and $2\ 4\ 2 \div 1,0\ 0\ 0 = 0\ .2\ 4\ 2$

More work to do...

1) $6\ 5\ 2 \div 1\ 0\ 0 =$

2) $4\ 7 \div 1\ 0\ 0 =$

3) $3,0\ 6\ 8 \div 1\ 0\ 0 =$

4) $1\ 2,9\ 4\ 3 \div 1,0\ 0\ 0 =$

5) $5\ 7\ 2 \div 1,0\ 0\ 0 =$

6) $3\ 0\ 1 \div 1,0\ 0\ 0 =$

> The important thing is to make sure you put decimal point in the right place. The order of the numbers doesn't change!

> Answers on page 138

Some of these division sums aren't easy, but you have to follow the rules {carefully}!

You can get confused with all those ZEROS!

So, here's a game you can play which makes

LONG MULTIPLICATION easier...!

Here's a sum.

$$2,000 \times 500$$

Do you think this one is difficult? Think again!

It's easy! If either number (or both) end in zeros, just add on the zeros to the answer!

2000 ends in three zeros. 500 ends in two zeros

So add FIVE zeros altogether to the answer...

Then 2 x 5 = 10, so the answer is 10 000 00!

$$2,000 \times 500 \over 1,000,000$$

(One million!)

Mr Prentice is making bad jokes again!

I've told you a million times - don't exaggerate!

Sadly, his jokes aren't getting any better!

I can do the same sort of thing when I'm dividing!

Look at   20 | 600   It looks difficult, but it isn't!

I can take off a zero from 20, and a zero from 600, so

20 | 600 becomes 2 | 60 so the answer is 30!

It's all about controlling the zeros ₒₒₒ OOO!

I have to do these.   Answers on page 138.

a)   300   b)   4,000   c)   200
   × 300   ×   50   × 70
   _____   _____   _____

   _____   _____   _____

d) 30 | 90   e) 400 | 800   f) 80 | 1,600

There are two **BIG** problems that I have -

1. The next school maths test is coming up, and
2. something else that is far, far worse -
   Maisie has gone missing!

She went out through the cat-flap
last night, and there's **NO** sign
of her this morning!

I should have been allowed to stay home to look for Maisie, but I wasn't allowed to...

so I had to do the dreaded **Maths Test**

Every month, there's another (school maths test).
Mr. Campbell is SOOO predictable!

Well, this month my test was...

...not brilliant,

but a lot better than before!!

...And Mr Campbell wrote

(in red ink!) Much Better!

This time I didn't need to hide

my maths book from mum.

She was even quite pleased with me!

So far, so good!

But there is still no sign of Maisie...

She's been gone for nearly a whole day!

There's no sign of her anywhere.

$$\begin{array}{r} 6\ 9 \\ 7\ 5 \\ \hline 4 \end{array} \ x$$

$$\begin{array}{r} 4\ 3\ 8 \\ x\quad\ 8 \\ \hline 3\ 5\ 0\ 4 \end{array} \checkmark$$

2

$$\begin{array}{r} 6\ 7 \\ x\quad 9 \\ \hline 6\ 0\ 3 \end{array} \checkmark$$

Much Better!

$$\frac{6}{10}$$

Maisie's back!

Maisie just came back in, through the :cat-flap:... !!

She headed for her food, and ate and ate. She was {cross}!

And then she went straight in front of the fire, and fell |fast asleep!|

That's the the (problem) with {cats}...

They disappear, then come back, and they NEVER actually :explain: where they've been all that time !

I have |no idea| where she's been all day, or what she got up to all that time...

?

I think it was Prento who drove her out, because he was here when she {disappeared}!

I think she must really HATE Maths!

Otherwise, Life seems to getting a bit easier!

Mr Prentice is back with more **DIVISION** !

(And Maisie has gone out of the room in disgust).

He says some division sums just leave a **REMAINDER**!

Look at this sum:

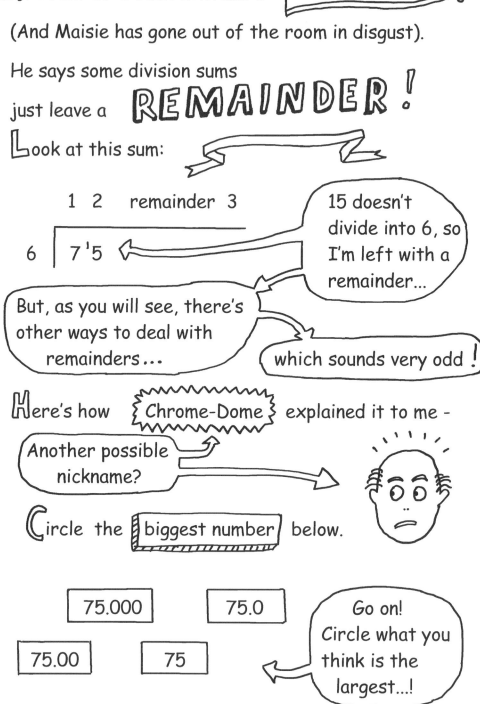

1 2   remainder 3

6 | 7 '5

15 doesn't divide into 6, so I'm left with a remainder...

But, as you will see, there's other ways to deal with remainders...

which sounds very odd !

Here's how {Chrome-Dome} explained it to me -

Another possible nickname?

Circle the **biggest number** below.

75.000

75.0

75.00

75

Go on! Circle what you think is the largest...!

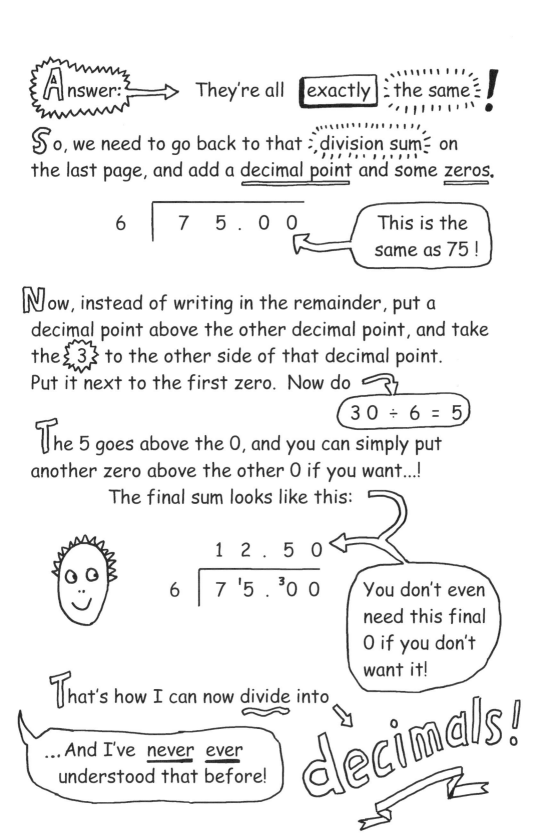

Answer: ⟶ They're all | exactly | the same !

So, we need to go back to that division sum on the last page, and add a decimal point and some zeros.

$$6 \overline{\smash{\big)}\, 7 \ 5 \ . \ 0 \ 0}$$

This is the same as 75 !

Now, instead of writing in the remainder, put a decimal point above the other decimal point, and take the 3 to the other side of that decimal point. Put it next to the first zero. Now do

30 ÷ 6 = 5

The 5 goes above the 0, and you can simply put another zero above the other 0 if you want...!

The final sum looks like this:

$$6 \overline{\smash{\big)}\, 7 \, {}^1 5 \ . \ {}^3 0 \ 0} = 1 \ 2 \ . \ 5 \ 0$$

You don't even need this final 0 if you don't want it!

That's how I can now divide into

...And I've never ever understood that before!

decimals!

61

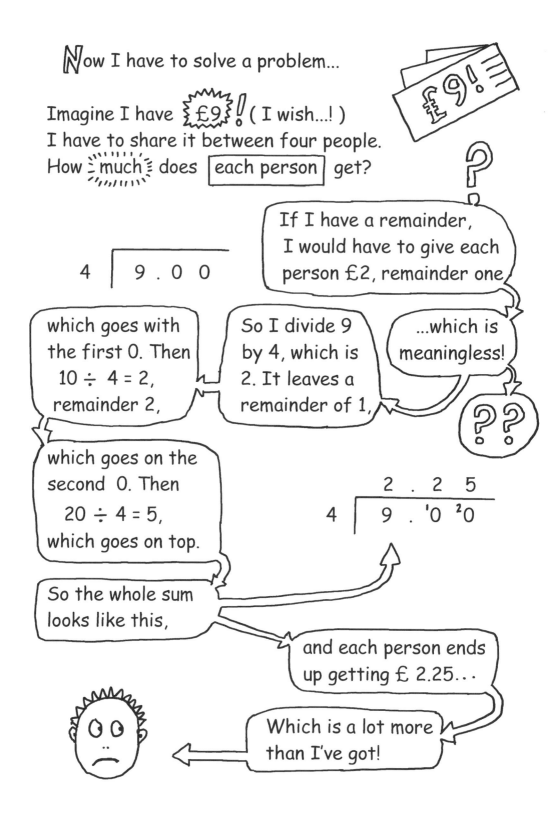

Now I have to solve a problem...

Imagine I have £9! (I wish...!)
I have to share it between four people.
How much does each person get?

4 | 9 . 0 0

If I have a remainder, I would have to give each person £2, remainder one

which goes with the first O. Then 10 ÷ 4 = 2, remainder 2,

So I divide 9 by 4, which is 2. It leaves a remainder of 1,

...which is meaningless!

which goes on the second O. Then 20 ÷ 4 = 5, which goes on top.

2 . 2 5
4 | 9 . '0 ²0

So the whole sum looks like this,

and each person ends up getting £ 2.25...

Which is a lot more than I've got!

I know what is going to come next! **Homework!**
There's always something _extra_ that I have to do!

The first one has the | decimals | I need —
the rest I will have to do {myself}...!

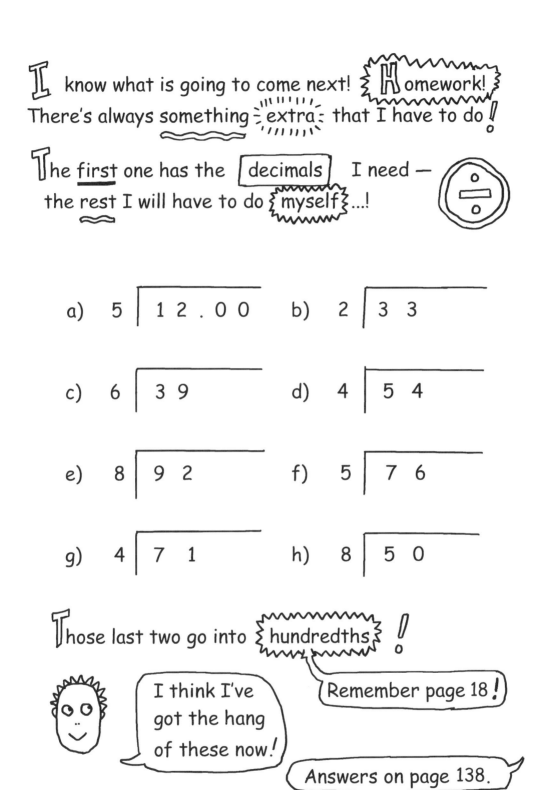

a) 5 | 1 2 . 0 0   b) 2 | 3 3

c) 6 | 3 9   d) 4 | 5 4

e) 8 | 9 2   f) 5 | 7 6

g) 4 | 7 1   h) 8 | 5 0

Those last two go into {hundredths}!

I think I've got the hang of these now!

Remember page 18!

Answers on page 138.

Sooo, I can now divide into {decimals}!
(Which for me is a pretty good achievement!)
Baldy - head says that while we're looking at
{decimals}, we might as well look at
adding and subtracting decimals as well.

He says it's not difficult!

It's only because so many people get them wrong!

But he's said that before!

Here's three examples -

Do them here!

1. Add 28 and 5.63

2. Subtract 0.83 from 60

3. Decrease 5.07 by 0.7

Answers on the next page!

Don't cheat!

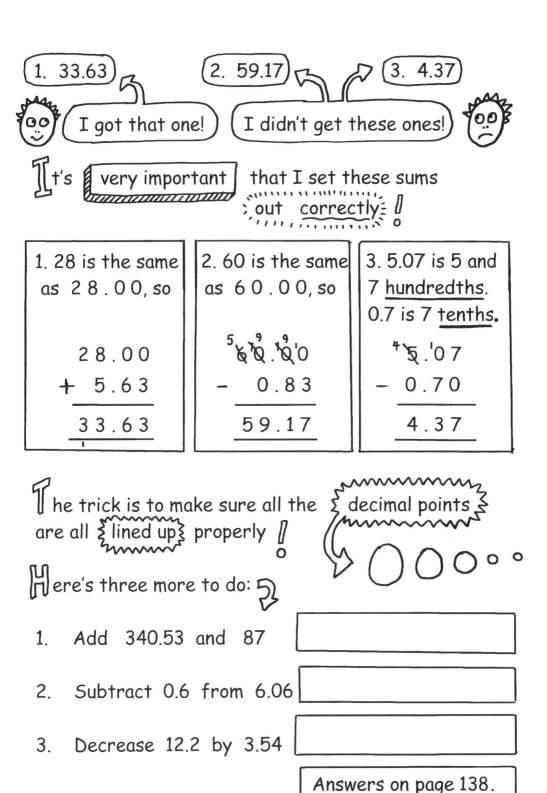

1. 33.63   2. 59.17   3. 4.37

I got that one!   I didn't get these ones!

It's very important that I set these sums out correctly!

1. 28 is the same as 28.00, so	2. 60 is the same as 60.00, so	3. 5.07 is 5 and 7 hundredths. 0.7 is 7 tenths.
28.00 + 5.63 = 33.63	60.00 - 0.83 = 59.17	5.07 - 0.70 = 4.37

The trick is to make sure all the decimal points are all lined up properly!

Here's three more to do:

1. Add 340.53 and 87

2. Subtract 0.6 from 6.06

3. Decrease 12.2 by 3.54

Answers on page 138.

Here's another quiz using DECIMALS!

1. Look at the numbers below:

Decide which of the numbers below do NOT change their value if the zeroes are not written...!

3004   0.56   4.06

2.60   108   5072

Circle all the numbers that change value. How many did you find?

2. Now try to sort this one out...!

Write down a number between 4.5 and 4.6

(You have to think about this one!)

3. This one is even harder!

What do you get when you subtract seventy-five
And six tenths from two hundred and fifty-four?

? ? ?

Answers over page. (Don't peek!)

66

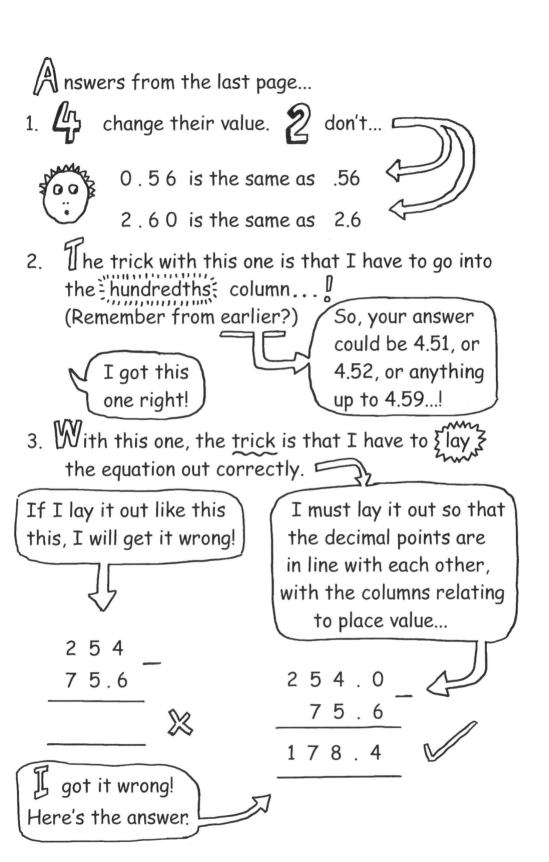

Answers from the last page...

1. **4** change their value. **2** don't...

0.56 is the same as .56

2.60 is the same as 2.6

2. The trick with this one is that I have to go into the hundredths column...!
(Remember from earlier?)

I got this one right!

So, your answer could be 4.51, or 4.52, or anything up to 4.59...!

3. With this one, the trick is that I have to lay the equation out correctly.

If I lay it out like this this, I will get it wrong!

I must lay it out so that the decimal points are in line with each other, with the columns relating to place value...

```
2 5 4
7 5.6  -
───────
```

```
2 5 4 . 0
    7 5 . 6  -
─────────
1 7 8 . 4
```

I got it wrong! Here's the answer.

I tried those questions out on { Mum. }

She didn't have a [clue]!
So I had to explain it to her...!
I'm not sure she understood...!
Even after I had explained how to get all the answers!!

Baldie tells me that we have to learn to put

[DECIMALS] in order!

Here's a TRICKY question. ⟹ Write

these numbers in order from { smallest } to { biggest... }

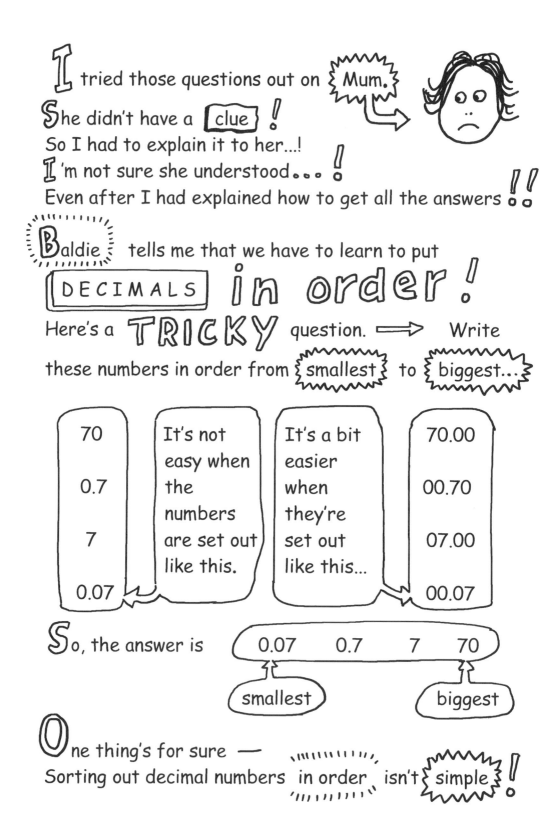

70	It's not easy when the numbers are set out like this.	It's a bit easier when they're set out like this...	70.00
0.7			00.70
7			07.00
0.07			00.07

So, the answer is (0.07   0.7   7   70)

smallest   biggest

One thing's for sure —
Sorting out decimal numbers in order isn't { simple }!

Here's a couple I have to do.

Write these in order, from {smallest} to {biggest.}

1)   330   0.33   33   3.3 → | | | | |
|---|---|---|---|

2)   800   0.8   80   8 → | | | | |
|---|---|---|---|

Now I have to write mixed decimal numbers in order!

I have to check where the decimal point is...

3)   48   0.5   0.09   7 → | | | | |
|---|---|---|---|

4)   0.56   6.5   0.8   26 → | | | | |
|---|---|---|---|

Some of those were difficult! (Answers on page 138.)

Another way of doing it is by looking at decimals in

terms of {NUMBER LINES} like the one below.

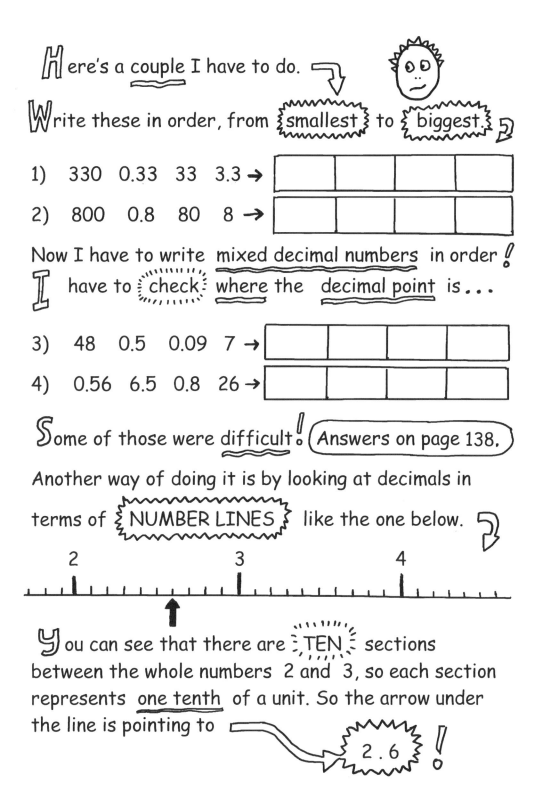

$y$ou can see that there are TEN sections between the whole numbers 2 and 3, so each section represents one tenth of a unit. So the arrow under the line is pointing to — 2.6!

69

Look at this number line.

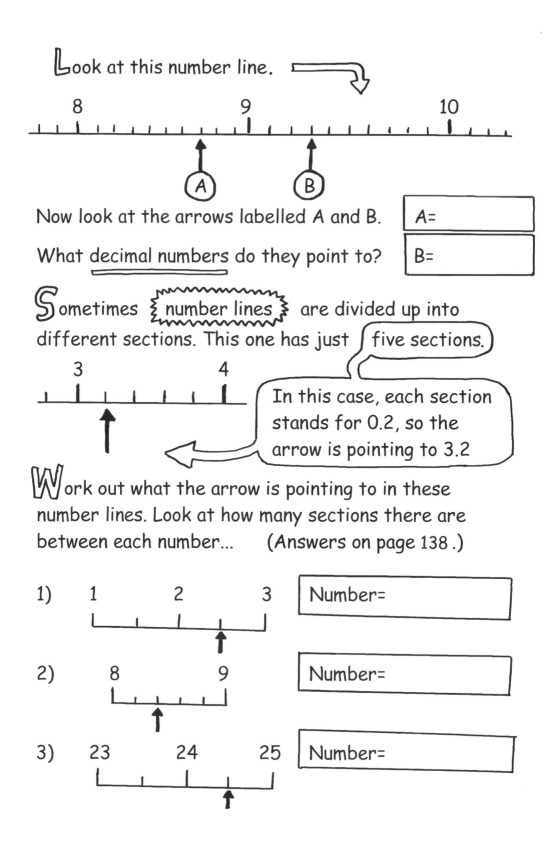

8   9   10

Now look at the arrows labelled A and B.

What decimal numbers do they point to?

A=

B=

Sometimes number lines are divided up into different sections. This one has just five sections.

3   4

In this case, each section stands for 0.2, so the arrow is pointing to 3.2

Work out what the arrow is pointing to in these number lines. Look at how many sections there are between each number... (Answers on page 138.)

1)   1   2   3   Number=

2)   8   9   Number=

3)   23   24   25   Number=

I _think_ I got those right, but they're not easy!

_L_ inked to this is ➩ DECIMAL NUMBER
(Which Mr P says
can be difficult...) SEQUENCES!

Here's an example.
What is the next number in this sequence?

2.4	2.6	2.8	3.0	?

These numbers are going up by 0.2 each time,
so the next number in this sequence is 3.2 !

_N_ ow work out the next number in these sequences, by
working out how much each number is increasing by...

1)	3.5	4.0	4.5	5.0 →

2)	2.5	2.8	3.1	3.4 →

3)	8.7	9.1	9.5	9.9 →

4)	15.7	15.9	16.1	→

5)	5.7	5.4	5.1	4.8 →

_N_ umber 5 is different to the others. Did you notice?
This time the numbers are decreasing, and I had to
subtract the numbers ! (Answers on page 139...)

71

I must admit, at this point I'm ‖ fed up ‖ with

OOo. [DECIMAL POINTS!] .oOO

Sometimes MATHS just gets on top of me,

... and I want to SCREAM !!

So I hereby declare that this page is a completely

MATHS-FREE zONE !

... and {NO} Mathematics will ever be on it !

I may ░add░ more pages with ░NO░ maths

(+) in the FUTURE as well...

It's all very well if I end up being

TOP OF THE CLASS

... but it's hard work getting there... !

So, if you ever get ░fed up░ with too much maths,

just come back to... {THIS PAGE} !!

I am also going to have to do something about Mr Prentice's **bad jokes !**

The fact that I don't { laugh } at any of them should give him some sort of a **HINT !**

I need to { learn } from **Maisie !**

She's laid back...
he just takes it easy...
he doesn't worry about anything...

(except for **FOOD !**)

Which is a little bit like **BOB**
... except that he likes **MATHS**
and { hates } **CatS... !**

A couple of weeks ago,

| MAISIE | dug her claws

into

him !

I'm sure he was doing something nasty to upset her !

Very sadly, back to | mathematics | on this page!

Mr P. is back! He says that decimals are all about

looking at numbers | in between | whole numbers.

For instance, (3.5) is an amount between (3) and (4).

Another way of looking at numbers in between

whole numbers is FRACTIONS!

It's just a different way of saying the same thing!

This is a FRACTION. So are these! $\frac{2}{3}$ $\frac{5}{6}$ $\frac{7}{8}$ $\frac{1}{3}$

The top bit is called the Numerator.
It tells you how many bits we're looking at.

The bottom bit is called the Denominator.
It's how many bits there are altogether.

There's always TWO parts to every fraction!

This one means the same as 1 divided by 2

I'm not sure why we need two different systems...

... but that seems to be the way LIFE is!!

Fraction **B**ars help to show what is going on.

This fraction bar shows $\frac{3}{4}$ or three quarters.

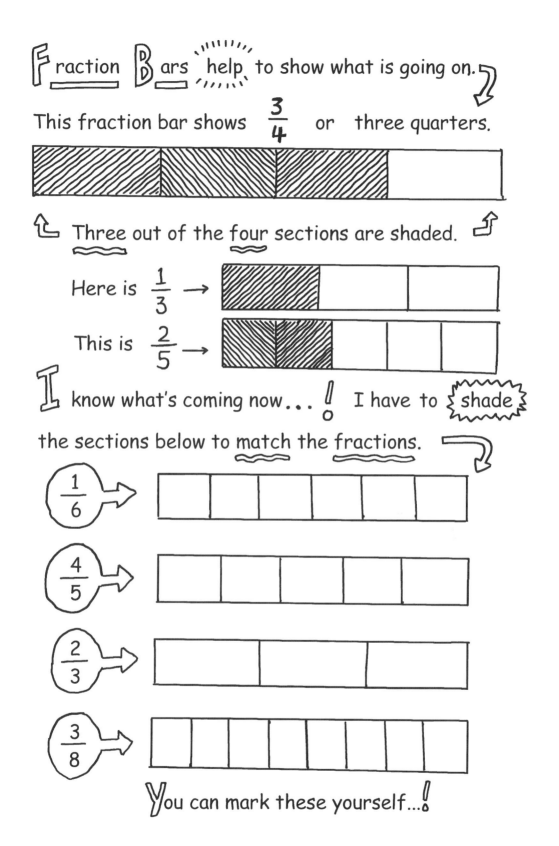

Three out of the four sections are shaded.

Here is $\frac{1}{3}$ →

This is $\frac{2}{5}$ →

I know what's coming now... ! I have to { shade }

the sections below to match the fractions.

$\frac{1}{6}$ ⇒

$\frac{4}{5}$ ⇒

$\frac{2}{3}$ ⇒

$\frac{3}{8}$ ⇒

You can mark these yourself...!

They were fairly *easy*...! ———>

But this time I've got to work out what *fraction* each { Fraction Bar } represents...

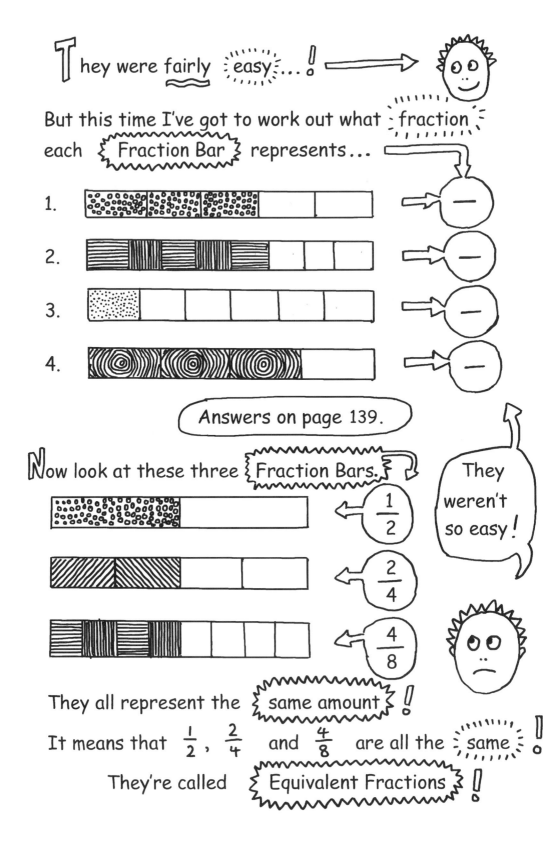

1. (—)

2. (—)

3. (—)

4. (—)

(Answers on page 139.)

Now look at these three { Fraction Bars. }

$\frac{1}{2}$

$\frac{2}{4}$

$\frac{4}{8}$

They weren't so easy!

They all represent the { same amount } !

It means that $\frac{1}{2}$, $\frac{2}{4}$ and $\frac{4}{8}$ are all the *same*!

They're called { Equivalent Fractions } !

Equivalent Fractions might look {different},
but they just represent fractions that are EQUAL.
An equivalent fraction can be made by multiplying
or dividing the [top] and [bottom] by same number.

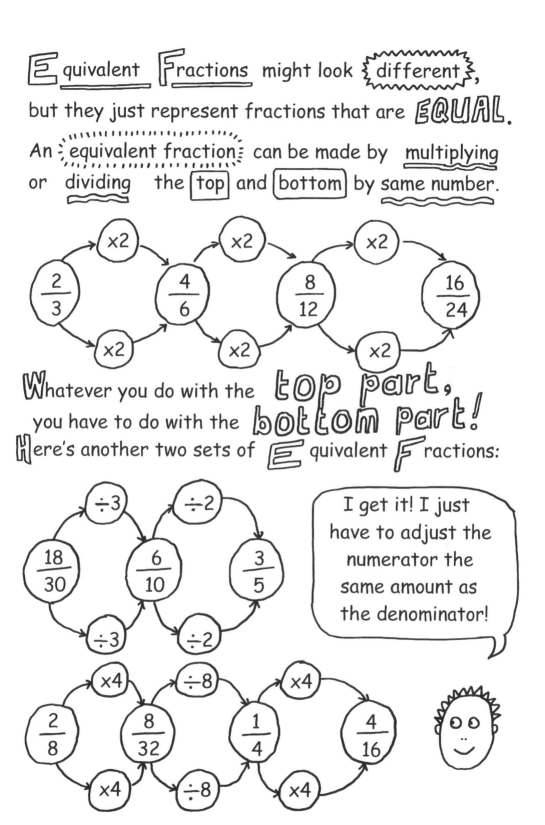

Whatever you do with the top part,
you have to do with the bottom part!
Here's another two sets of Equivalent Fractions:

I get it! I just
have to adjust the
numerator the
same amount as
the denominator!

When an Equivalent Fraction gets

as LOW as it can go, it is called a fraction in its

Lowest Terms!

So, $\frac{4}{20}$ in its lowest terms is $\frac{1}{5}$ It can't go any lower than this!

Surprise! Surprise! I have further homework!

Bring these fractions down to their lowest terms.

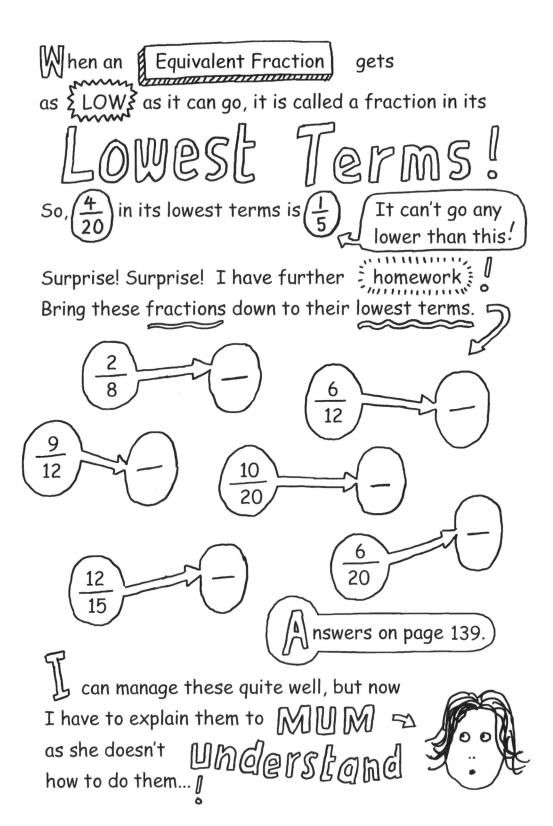

$\frac{2}{8} \rightarrow \boxed{-}$

$\frac{6}{12} \rightarrow \boxed{-}$

$\frac{9}{12} \rightarrow \boxed{-}$

$\frac{10}{20} \rightarrow \boxed{-}$

$\frac{12}{15} \rightarrow \boxed{-}$

$\frac{6}{20} \rightarrow \boxed{-}$

Answers on page 139.

I can manage these quite well, but now

I have to explain them to MUM

as she doesn't understand

how to do them...!

Well, I've got some GOOD news!

By coincidence, Mr Campbell is teaching us DECIMALS and FRACTIONS!

I think everybody in the class is finding it VERY HARD WORK!

But - he spoke to me at the end of class...

Jack! You're doing very well with decimals and fractions!

Yes! It's not too difficult!

I said that bit very loudly so that the rest of the class could hear me!

Well done! Keep up the good work!

I'm sure I saw a few of the others in the class looking angrily at me!

I may not be bottom of the class any more!

The only trouble with all that is, now I have to keep on being good at maths!

79

The most (surprising) thing is, Mr Campbell has never been **nice** about my **Maths** before **!**

Now I have a <u>problem</u>. Do I tell **Mum** what { Mr Campbell } has said to me... **??**

I'm sure she will just say that it's all because I've been <u>seeing</u> { <u>Prento.</u> }

And then I would have to see him

FOR EVER MORE.

So, maybe it's best if I keep it to myself...

(... for the moment, anyway...!)

But it still gives me lots of encouragement **!**

And I've made up a good **joke** as well **!!**

I think I understand fractions now, Mr. Campbell...!

Good! Did you do all your homework then?

I only needed to do half of it!

Oh, well...!! Mr. Prentice is back!

And he's still got FRACTIONS on the brain!

Here's my next piece of work. → It's a game!

Which of these is the biggest? $\frac{1}{4}$ $\frac{3}{8}$ or $\frac{1}{2}$?

What you have to do is change each fraction around so that the DENOMINATORS are the same!

8 is the biggest denominator, and (4) and (2) divide into (8), so they have to change.

$\frac{1}{4}$ becomes $\frac{2}{8}$ and $\frac{1}{2}$ becomes $\frac{4}{8}$

That means the fractions become $\frac{2}{8}$, $\frac{3}{8}$ and $\frac{4}{8}$

Therefore, $\frac{4}{8}$, which is the same as $\frac{1}{2}$,

is the BIGGEST!

My biggest problem is that I have too much maths to do!

So now it's my turn! I knew it was coming...!

I have to find out which of each of these sets of fractions is the { B I G G E S T } one!

I've got a bit of help with the <u>first</u> one, but not with any of the others!

The biggest one is... ?

1. $\dfrac{2}{3}$ $\dfrac{5}{6}$ $\dfrac{1}{2}$ $=$ $\dfrac{}{6}$ $\dfrac{}{6}$ $\dfrac{}{6}$ $\Rightarrow$ $\dfrac{}{}$

2. $\dfrac{3}{4}$ $\dfrac{5}{8}$ $\dfrac{1}{2}$ $=$ $\dfrac{}{}$ $\dfrac{}{}$ $\dfrac{}{}$ $\Rightarrow$ $\dfrac{}{}$

3. $\dfrac{3}{5}$ $\dfrac{1}{2}$ $\dfrac{7}{10}$ $=$ $\dfrac{}{}$ $\dfrac{}{}$ $\dfrac{}{}$ $\Rightarrow$ $\dfrac{}{}$

4. $\dfrac{1}{6}$ $\dfrac{3}{12}$ $\dfrac{1}{3}$ $=$ $\dfrac{}{}$ $\dfrac{}{}$ $\dfrac{}{}$ $\Rightarrow$ $\dfrac{}{}$

5. $\dfrac{7}{8}$ $\dfrac{3}{4}$ $\dfrac{13}{16}$ $=$ $\dfrac{}{}$ $\dfrac{}{}$ $\dfrac{}{}$ $\Rightarrow$ $\dfrac{}{}$

That <u>last</u> one was very <u>hard!</u>   **A**nswers on page 139.

Mr P says what we're doing here is : finding : the

{ C O M M O N   D E N O M I N A T O R ! }

Now I have to find fractions of WHOLE AMOUNTS!

But it's not too difficult!

At least, that's what Baldy-Head says!

What you have to do is:

Divide the amount by the denominator, and multiply the amount by the numerator.
It doesn't matter which one you do first!

So, $\dfrac{2}{3}$ of 12 = 8

12 divided by 3 is 4, then 4 x 2 = 8

I know it sounds complicated, but it's not!

Here's my homework. I have to work these out.

1. $\dfrac{3}{4}$ of 20 = ☐

2. $\dfrac{5}{8}$ of 16 = ☐

3. $\dfrac{1}{6}$ of 24 = ☐

4. $\dfrac{4}{5}$ of 40 = ☐

5. $\dfrac{7}{8}$ of 32 = ☐

Answers on page 139.

I've decided that it's time to give BOB a TEST!

He thinks he's good at MATHS!

So I've worked out a | Fractions Test | for him ...

Which of these : fractions : are the same as ↳ ($\frac{1}{2}$) ?

Shade in all the fractions in the box below

that are the same.

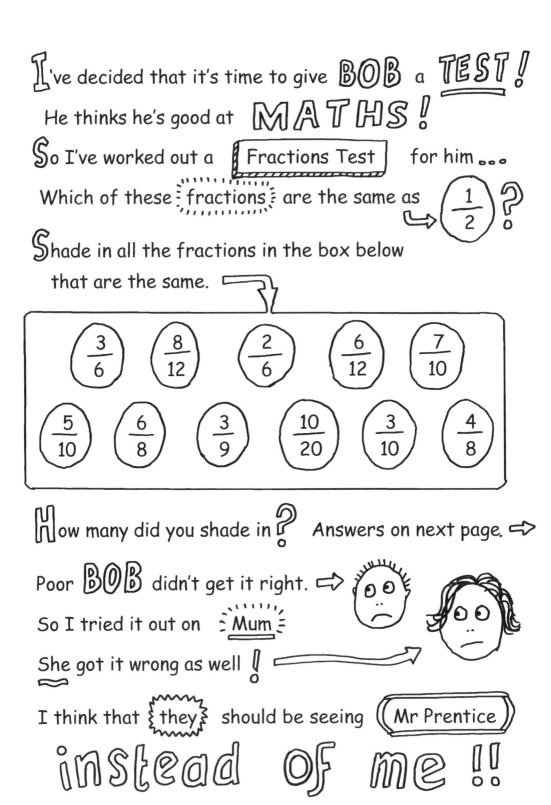

$\frac{3}{6}$ $\frac{8}{12}$ $\frac{2}{6}$ $\frac{6}{12}$ $\frac{7}{10}$

$\frac{5}{10}$ $\frac{6}{8}$ $\frac{3}{9}$ $\frac{10}{20}$ $\frac{3}{10}$ $\frac{4}{8}$

How many did you shade in? Answers on next page. ⇨

Poor BOB didn't get it right. ⇨

So I tried it out on : Mum :

She got it wrong as well!

I think that {they} should be seeing ((Mr Prentice))

instead of me !!

In the {Fractions Test} on the last page,

BOB should have shaded 5 fractions !

$$\frac{3}{6}, \frac{6}{12}, \frac{5}{10}, \frac{10}{20} \text{ and } \frac{4}{8} \text{ are all the same as } \frac{1}{2} !$$

Mr Prentice is back - and I think MUM has said something to him - because I've been set a TEST that is far more DIFFICULT !

I have to {fill in} all the blank boxes.

The only hint he's given me. → Whatever you do to the top line, you also have to do to the bottom line.

1. $$\frac{4}{12} = \frac{\square}{6} = \frac{8}{\square} = \frac{\square}{3}$$

2. $$\frac{3}{5} = \frac{\square}{15} = \frac{18}{\square} = \frac{6}{\square}$$

3. $$\frac{2}{8} = \frac{\square}{40} = \frac{5}{\square} = \frac{\square}{4}$$

Answers on page 139

FRACTIONS and DECIMALS

are two ways of saying...

the **same thing!**

According to 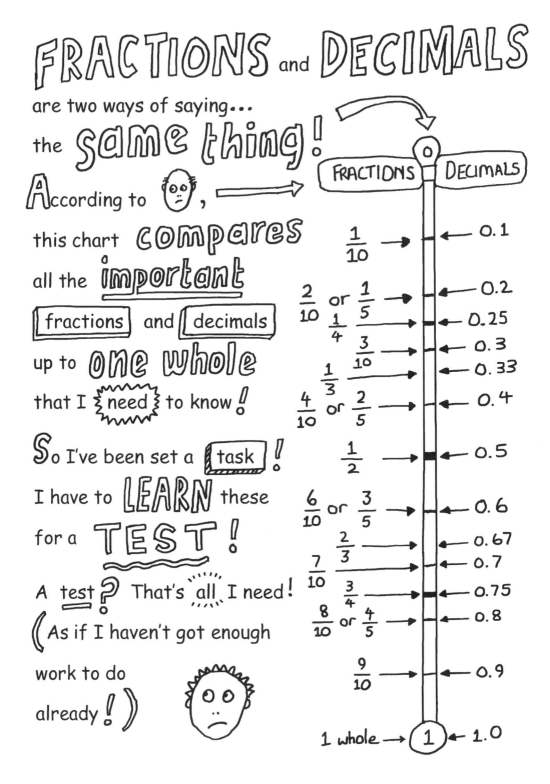,

this chart **compares**

all the **important**

[fractions] and [decimals]

up to **one whole**

that I {need} to know!

So I've been set a [task]!

I have to **LEARN** these

for a **TEST!**

A test? That's all I need!

(As if I haven't got enough

work to do

already!)

FRACTIONS	DECIMALS
$\frac{1}{10}$	0.1
$\frac{2}{10}$ or $\frac{1}{5}$	0.2
$\frac{1}{4}$	0.25
$\frac{3}{10}$	0.3
$\frac{1}{3}$	0.33
$\frac{4}{10}$ or $\frac{2}{5}$	0.4
$\frac{1}{2}$	0.5
$\frac{6}{10}$ or $\frac{3}{5}$	0.6
$\frac{2}{3}$	0.67
$\frac{7}{10}$	0.7
$\frac{3}{4}$	0.75
$\frac{8}{10}$ or $\frac{4}{5}$	0.8
$\frac{9}{10}$	0.9
1 whole → 1	1.0

Just when I thought I understood all this stuff,
Mr Prentice has added something else...
He has told me that, as well as fractions and decimals, there's YET ANOTHER way of looking at numbers less than one whole.

PERCENTAGES!

He says PER CENT is Latin for out of 100.
So a percentage means an amount out of 100...
(I think he must be making some of this up! Latin?)

And this sign is a short way of writing it!

He says it's easy to understand, but he says that about everything we do...!

So why do we bother to use percentages ?

Percentages are simpler to use than fractions. They can be compared more easily. They're all around us...

Hmmm...!

Here's all the important {percentages} along with the equivalent fractions and decimals that I need to know.

means the same.

FRACTIONS	DECIMALS	PERCENTAGES
one tenth ⇒ $\frac{1}{10}$ =	0.1 =	10%
one fifth ⇒ $\frac{2}{10}$ or $\frac{1}{5}$ =	0.2 =	20%
one quarter ⇒ $\frac{1}{4}$ =	0.25 =	25%
three tenths ⇒ $\frac{3}{10}$ =	0.3 =	30%
one third ⇒ $\frac{1}{3}$ =	0.33 =	33.3%
two fifths ⇒ $\frac{4}{10}$ or $\frac{2}{5}$ =	0.4 =	40%
one half ⇒ $\frac{1}{2}$ =	0.5 =	50%
three fifths ⇒ $\frac{6}{10}$ or $\frac{3}{5}$ =	0.6 =	60%
two thirds ⇒ $\frac{2}{3}$ =	0.66 =	66.6%
seven tenths ⇒ $\frac{7}{10}$ =	0.7 =	70%
three quarters ⇒ $\frac{3}{4}$ =	0.75 =	75%
four fifths ⇒ $\frac{8}{10}$ or $\frac{4}{5}$ =	0.8 =	80%
nine tenths ⇒ $\frac{9}{10}$ =	0.9 =	90%
one whole ⇒ 1 =	1.0 =	100%

My tutor → says that ⦂last page⦂ is one of the { most important } pages I'll { ever } need to know!

He says it's easy to convert decimals to percentages.

Just multiply the decimal by ⇒ 100!

For instance, 0.3 × 100 = 30%

Converting fractions to percentages isn't hard either.

Work out the fraction, then use the last page to work out the { percentage. } Here's an example.

What percentage of this shape is shaded?

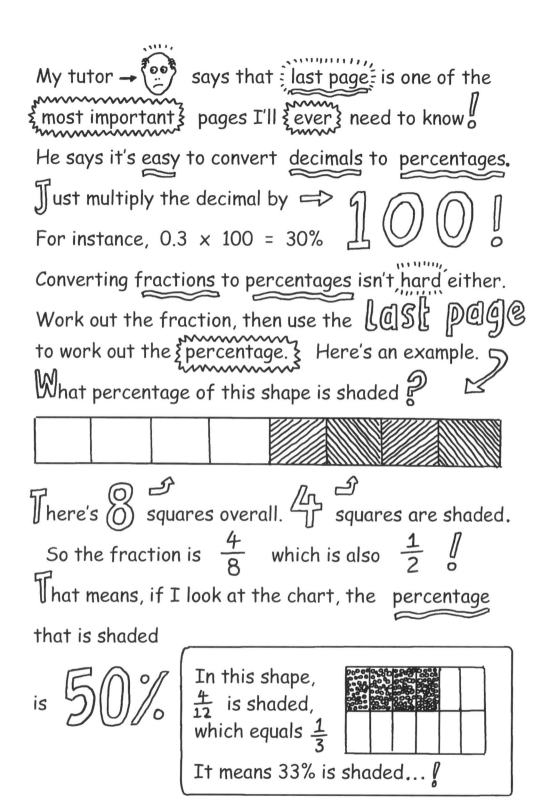

There's 8 squares overall. 4 squares are shaded.

So the fraction is $\frac{4}{8}$ which is also $\frac{1}{2}$!

That means, if I look at the chart, the percentage

that is shaded

is 50%

In this shape, $\frac{4}{12}$ is shaded, which equals $\frac{1}{3}$

It means 33% is shaded... !

$\mathbb{I}$ knew it! $\mathbb{I}$ have homework to do... !

$\mathbb{F}$ irst, I have to convert { decimals } to { percentages. }

1) Write these <u>decimals</u> as <u>percentages</u>. ⤵

     a)   0.2 = [%]   b) 0.75 = [%]

     c)   0.33 = [%]   d) 0.9   = [%]

$\mathbb{T}$ hey're easy enough! $\mathbb{N}$ ow for the next test!

2) What { percentage } of these shapes are [shaded] ?

a)

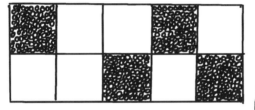

     = [%]

     (Answers on page 140.)

b) = [%] c)

     = [%]

d)   e)

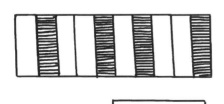

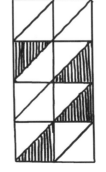

     = [%]   = [%]

$\mathbb{I}$ managed to get those [right]! I must {remember}

that a ⟨percentage⟩ is an amount out of 100.

> 70% means 70 out of 100, or $\dfrac{70}{100}$

To change ⟨fractions⟩ to ⟨percentages⟩,
I have to change the <u>denominator</u> part of
the (fraction) to an amount out of <u>100</u>!

$\overset{\times 25}{\underset{\times 25}{\dfrac{3}{4}}} \quad \dfrac{75}{100} = \boxed{75\%}$

$\overset{\times 5}{\underset{\times 5}{\dfrac{16}{20}}} \quad \dfrac{80}{100} = \boxed{80\%}$

$\mathbb{N}$ow I have to change these <u>fractions</u> to <u>percentages</u>.

1) $\dfrac{10}{50} = $ [ ] %

2) $\dfrac{20}{25} = $ [ ] %

3) $\dfrac{15}{20} = $ [ ] %

4) $\dfrac{3}{5} = $ [ ] %

5) $\dfrac{45}{50} = $ [ ] %

6) $\dfrac{6}{15} = $ [ ] %

> Answers on
> page 140.

> This is a very tough one.
> First it has to be divided by 3,
> and then multiplied by 20.

Mr P. says that one good thing about percentages is that it's easy to find the (percentage of an amount!

For instance, if I want to work out 20% of 60,

I just need to do two things...

1) Divide 60 by 10 = 6.

2) Multiply the answer by this bit of the %

So the answer is 6 × 2 = 12!   Easy!

Even if I want to find 70% of 25, it's fairly easy!

25 ÷ 10 = 2.5   2.5 × 7 = 17.5

More homework! Find the answers to these.

1) 30% of 50 =

2) 80% of 90 =

Another page that I can understand!

3) 40% of 120 =

4) 20% of 45 =

5) 70% of 30 =

Answers on page 140...

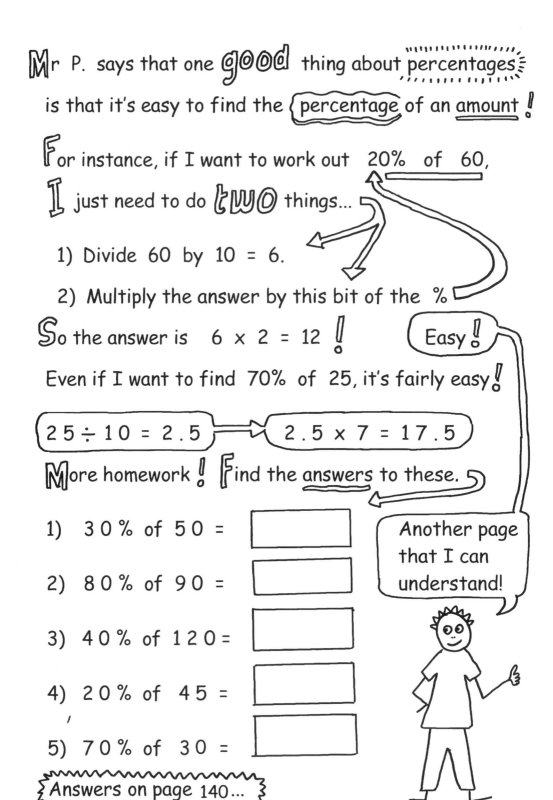

Ok! I can understand those, but **Maisie** isn't so **impressed!**

And... she's had a tough time in the past week or so.

She's had {run-ins} with **BOB** recently, and she hates {my tutor!}

Maybe that's why she {ran away} a week ago... ?!?

So, I'm trying to **pamper** her!

The only things she really likes are {food} and {sleep}

I'm giving her lots of extra **food**, anyway...

(**MUM** doesn't know about it!)

But I think she's getting (fat)!

And she gets enough **SLEEP!**

Anyway, there's a {bigger problem} coming up !!

It's another school **MATHS TEST!**

But there's {good news}! Mr Campbell has told me that it's all about Fractions, ½ 0.5 Decimals, and 50% Percentages! This time I {nearly} got FULL MARKS! I knew just about EVERYTHING!

And MUM found out... I had to leave my maths book lying around the house so that she saw it!

So it's nearly all {good news.}

Except that I still have to see Mr P. every week!

I tried to convince Mum that because my Maths was now so {good,} I don't have to see him any more...

(but I don't think I convinced her)!

And there's something coming up that is far worse than any {maths test.}

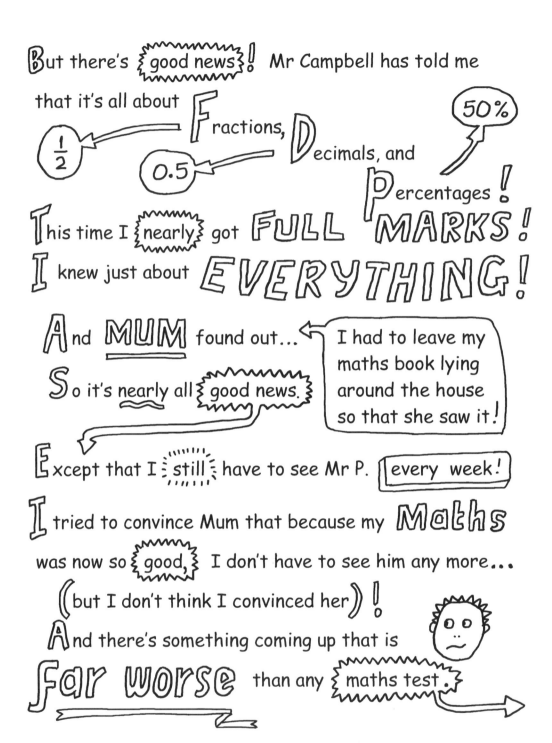

PARENTS' EVENING!

I have **never** had a {Parents' Evening} where
the teachers have said **NICE** things about me!
They all find :something horrible: to say about me...
It's usually about the lack of **EFFORT**
that I put into my [work.] ← The most critical
teacher is always
Mr Campbell !

...And I'm not allowed to go!
So when my **MUM**
came back home, I was {more} than worried !
I was **very, very, very worried...!**

But she didn't seem too :unhappy: overall.
She told me that some teachers said that I must
TRY much harder in the {classroom} !

Then she told me what Mr Campbell had said...!

Much improved!

Great test results!

...good knowledge of fractions...!

Very good effort.

Excellent!

...concentrates well in class...

Working hard!

There's a few {extra} comments I've added here that he **might not** have said, but you get the idea!

The :only thing: I was |worried about| was whether **MUM** had mentioned that I had a **TUTOR**, but she said she thought she'd better not mention it...!

So, for a {very} short time, I'm not in the bad books!

But, I'm also sure that :Mr Prentice: will get **ALL THE CREDIT!**

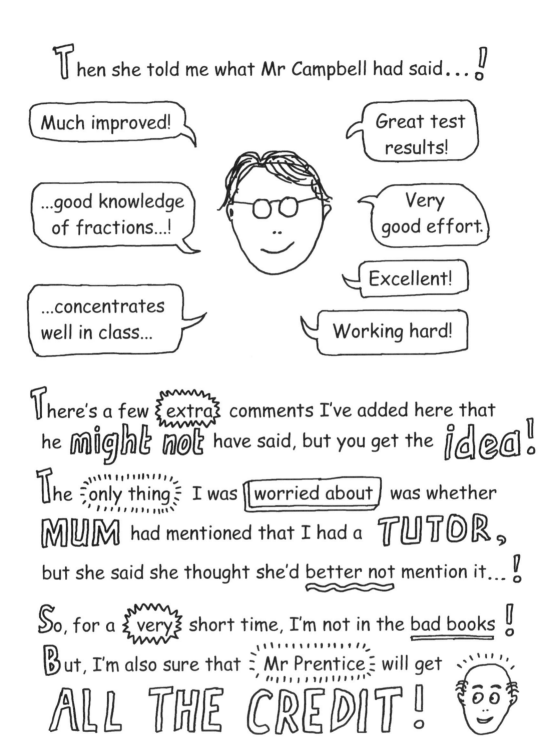

96

According to Mr. Prentice, we now have
to look at...

Factors...!

Well, he says that {FACTORS} are
whole numbers that are multiplied together to
produce another number.

The :original: numbers are the factors...
(... which doesn't help me much so far...)

Then he explained it this way.

Which tables are these numbers on?

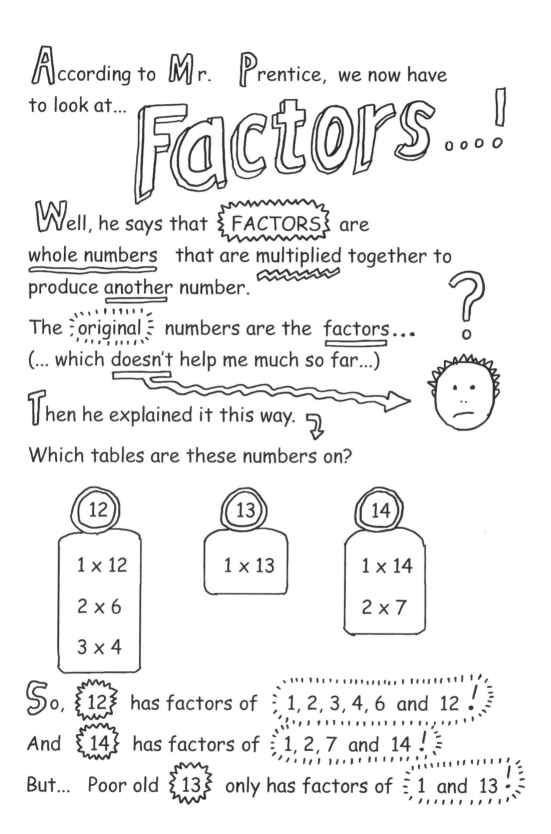

12

1 x 12

2 x 6

3 x 4

13

1 x 13

14

1 x 14

2 x 7

So, {12} has factors of : 1, 2, 3, 4, 6 and 12 !

And {14} has factors of : 1, 2, 7 and 14 !

But... Poor old {13} only has factors of : 1 and 13 !

97

S o... What about poor old **13** ?

Well, 13 is one of a set of numbers called

PRIME NUMBERS.

Prime Numbers are special, because they have

NO factors , except for 1 and the number itself !

(But more about them soon!)

Factors are useful things, according to ☞ because they will be involved in lots of things we will look at in the future...

I 've got more homework, and it's NOT easy .

Write down all the factors for each of the numbers below, by filling in the boxes next to each number. The number of boxes tells you how many factors each number has!

Answers on next page.

15 ☐ ☐ ☐ ☐

16 ☐ ☐ ☐ ☐ ☐

18 ☐ ☐ ☐ ☐ ☐ ☐

20 ☐ ☐ ☐ ☐ ☐ ☐

Did you get them all? I didn't!!

Factors of 15 are ① ③ ⑤ ⑮

Factors of 16 are ① ② ④ ⑧ ⑯

Factors of 18 are ① ② ③ ⑥ ⑨ ⑱

Factors of 20 are ① ② ④ ⑤ ⑩ ⑳

For instance, (1 × 16) (2 × 8) and (4 × 4) all equal 16,

and (1 × 20) (2 × 10) and (4 × 5) all equal 20.

Factor Pairs...

... are the names of these numbers...!

Here's another game. Find all the factor pairs of these numbers.

21
× 21
×

24
×
× 12
×
×

28
× 28
×
×

32
×
× 16
×

A few clues have been added! Answers on page 140.

35
×
×

Now comes the BIG question:

How do you {work out} if any number is a...

PRIME NUMBER?

You have to answer these questions:

● Is the number divisible by **2** ? Yes
(Is the number an even number?
(Does it end in 2, 4, 6, 8 or 0?)

If the answer is NO

● Is the number divisible by **3** ? Yes

If the answer is NO

● Is the number divisible by **5** ? Yes
(Does the number end in 0 or 5?)

If the answer is NO

● Is the number divisible by **7** ? Yes

If the answer to ANY of these numbers is YES, the number is NOT prime.

If the answer to {ALL} of these questions is NO,
The number is a ... {PRIME NUMBER!}

Important note: ②③ 5 and ⑦ are all
prime numbers!

The [Prime Number Rules] on the last page cover every number you can think of ...
— even very large numbers!

For instance, [146] is NOT PRIME, because it ends in a (6), so it is divisible by 2.

[2,355] is NOT PRIME because it ends in a 5, so it is on the (5) times table!

But (41) is PRIME because it is {not} on the (2) or (3) or (5) or (7) times tables... !

Here's a ·difficult· question. ⟹ Which numbers between (20) and (25) are ·Prime Numbers· ?

The way to sort this out is to look at all the numbers.

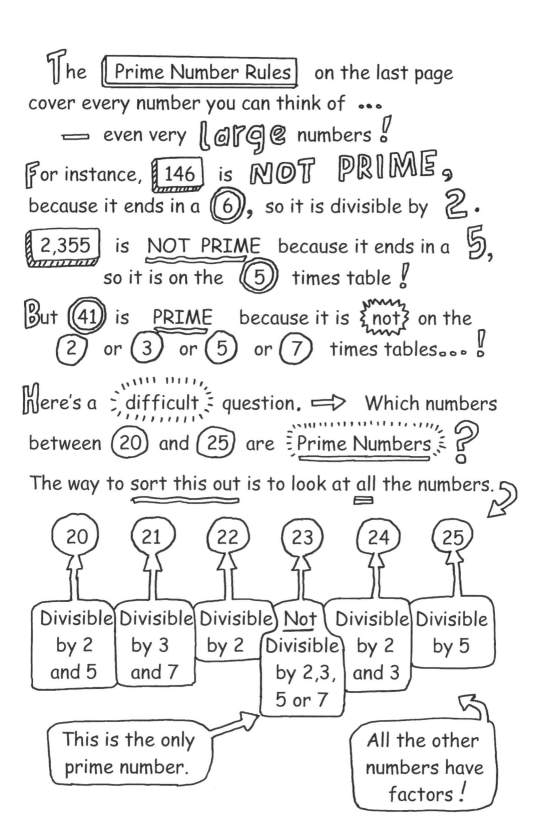

(20)	(21)	(22)	(23)	(24)	(25)

| Divisible by 2 and 5 | Divisible by 3 and 7 | Divisible by 2 | Not Divisible by 2,3, 5 or 7 | Divisible by 2 and 3 | Divisible by 5 |

This is the only prime number.

All the other numbers have factors!

101

Now I've got to do another TEST which involves prime numbers. It's not _not_ EASY at all ... !

1) Work out all the prime numbers between

30 and 40

Baldie has hinted that the best way to answer this is to cross out all the numbers that have FACTORS ... and then see what you're left with.

Here's a list of all of the candidates. →

(30) (31) (32) (33) (34) (35)

(36) (37) (38) (39) (40)

Which ones have NO factors? ☐ ☐

If you've crossed out the right ones, you should have just TWO that are LEFT!

2) Look at these numbers. How many are PRIME ?

51		44		47
	43		56	
42	48			53
	57		41	

(Answers on page 140.)

Here's another couple of {FUN} questions...!

Remember [prime numbers] are

not divisible by (2), (3), (5) and (7).

3) Write the next [prime number] after

a)   14 ⟹ ☐

b)   25 ⟹ ☐

c)   44 ⟹ ☐

Fun is Mr P's word!
   I think these
   questions are
anything but fun!

4)   Find one [prime number] between

a)   8 and 12 ⟹ ☐

b)   20 and 25 ⟹ ☐

5)   Find two [prime numbers] between

a)   4 and 9 → ☐ ☐

b)   60 and 68 → ☐ ☐

Answers on
page 140.

Well, as far as I am concerned, {FUN}
is not a word I would use to describe these questions!
   In fact, they're horrible...!

At school, (Mr Campbell) has been looking at prime numbers as well... !

He's given the {whole class} a big piece of paper with a list of every prime number from 1 to 200 for us to learn for a test...

... It sounds like very HARD WORK!

I was going to tell him that you don't need to learn them like that, but then I thought –

(I'll just keep it to myself!)

Anyway, MUM let something SLIP OUT by mistake!

I've found out Mr P's christian name!

It's LEO...!!

Which is fairly {odd} because he doesn't look like a LEO!

Leo is the name of a lion!

(Here's my new picture of him!)

PRIME NUM

2 3 5 7 11
19 23 29 31
43 47 53 59
67 71 73 79
91 97 101 1C
113 119 121 1
129 131 133
143 149 151

BUT... there's something wrong...

Lions have lots of HAIR !

That's BETTER! →

That looks much more like him !

And it gets EVEN better...

I came out TOP in the Prime Numbers Test !

Mr Campbell says he is very impressed

with my excellent learning skills !

(He thinks that I memorised the whole page !)

I'm quite tempted to tell him

how I really know how to work out prime numbers,

but then I'd have to tell him about my TUTOR...

so it might be BEST to keep quiet about it,

and tell NOBODY !

But at least I can tell MUM all about

my successful MATHS TEST !

Top of the class is *pretty good!*
It's *somewhere* I've never been before!
And at the moment *life* isn't too bad! *MUM* is pleased with my *progress!*
But... now I've got to

stay there!

And that's going to be *hard work!*

The trouble is, I'm going to have to ← *really study* to *stay* there...!

...And I *hate* working hard!

I think I learned to hate work from *MAISIE!*

She's laid back! She does *NO* work...
She just spends all day *fast asleep!*

I wish I could do that!

Mr P is back! I'd love to call him LEO...

... but I don't think I'd better ▭ just yet!

He says we have to look at ⬛ S Q U A R E numbers.

He says they're ⸝easy,⸜ but he {always} says that !

A SQUARE number is a number that is

multiplied by itself!

3 x 3 = 9, so 9 is a square number.

It can also be written as 3^2 = 9

Look at this square.

That little 2 means 'squared'!

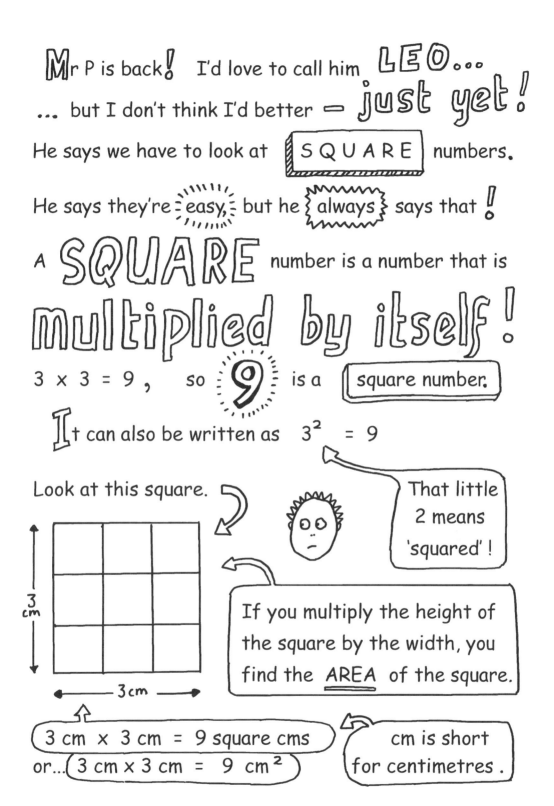

3
cm

3 cm

If you multiply the height of the square by the width, you find the AREA of the square.

3 cm x 3 cm = 9 square cms

or... 3 cm x 3 cm = 9 cm²

cm is short for centimetres.

Here's a list of all the SQUARE numbers...
(all the way up to 12 x 12).

(1) (4) (9) (16) (24) (36)

(49) (64) (81) (100) (121) (144)

According to (Mr Leo P.) this is an

important list

that I have to LEARN !

1 x 1 = 1, so 1 is a square number.

Now I have to learn about CUBE numbers...

A CUBE NUMBER is a number that is

⇒ multiplied by itself...

⇒ and then multiplied by itself ↗ again!

3 x 3 x 3 = 27, so 27 is a cube number.

It can also be written as 3^3 = 27

That little 3 means 'cubed' !

Now look at this CUBE...

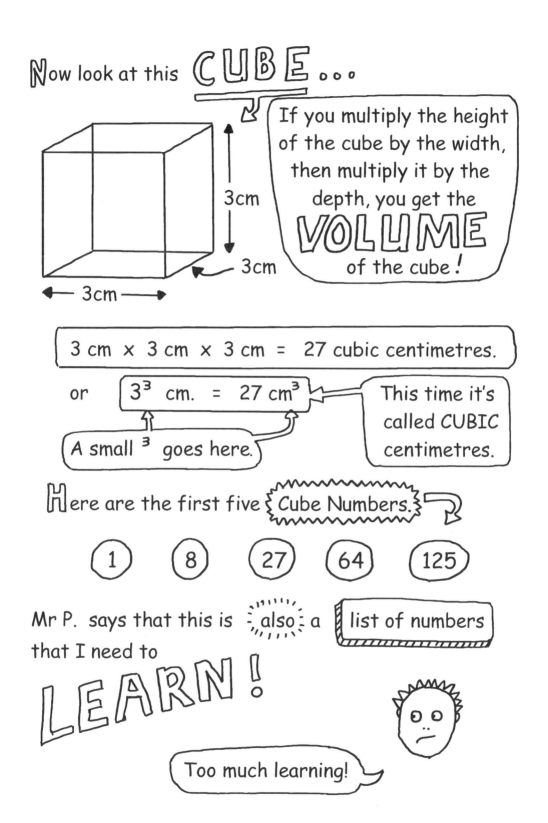

3cm

3cm

3cm

If you multiply the height of the cube by the width, then multiply it by the depth, you get the VOLUME of the cube!

3 cm x 3 cm x 3 cm = 27 cubic centimetres.

or 3^3 cm. = 27 cm^3

A small ^{3} goes here.

This time it's called CUBIC centimetres.

Here are the first five Cube Numbers.

1   8   27   64   125

Mr P. says that this is also a list of numbers that I need to

LEARN!

Too much learning!

109

I don't really understand AREA or VOLUME.

So here's how Leo the Lion explains it.

Think of the top surface of a table.

AREA is the measurement of something in {two} dimensions.

VOLUME is the measure-ment of something in {three} dimensions.

Think of how much a box holds.

But he says we will do more about that when we get to SHAPE and SPACE.

Now I've got more homework!

Look at all the {numbers} below.

Find {5} square numbers and {4} cube numbers from all the numbers below.

28 56 36 88 2
81 45 9 27
18 49 54 96 8
125 24 64

Answers on page 140.

Now I've got to answer these [questions.]
Fill in all the missing numbers...

1) $5^2 = 5 \times \boxed{} = \boxed{}$

2) $6^2 = \boxed{} \times \boxed{} = \boxed{}$

3) $8^2 = \boxed{} \times \boxed{} = \boxed{}$

4) $2^3 = \boxed{} \times 2 \times \boxed{} = \boxed{}$

5) $4^3 = \boxed{} \times \boxed{} \times \boxed{} = \boxed{}$

6) $5^3 = \boxed{} \times \boxed{} \times \boxed{} = \boxed{}$

7) Work out what 6^3 is. ⇒ $\boxed{}$

(not easy!)

8) Here's another *difficult* test.

Answers on page 141.

Look at the numbers below...

Which ones *add up* to make a {square number}?

Draw lines between ((two)) numbers so that they *add up* to make a *square number.*

6   11   8   18

5   3   28   7

(Every number should be used up!)

111

That last question was **hard work!**

This {Maths} business isn't **EASY...**

Mr P. told me <u>one</u> more thing about square numbers.

The **opposite** of a square number

is called a

SQUARE ROOT.

It sounds like something you <u>plant</u>! ⟹

√ (Here's the sign for a square root!)

So, if 8 x 8 = 64, then $\sqrt{64}$ = 8

Here's another little **TEST...**

Write the answers to these. ⟹

1) $\sqrt{25}$ = ☐   2) $\sqrt{49}$ = ☐

3) $\sqrt{36}$ = ☐   4) $\sqrt{81}$ = ☐

Those aren't <u>too bad</u>! (Answers on page 141 ...)

I realise I'm going to have to work {hard} to stay

near to the

TOP OF THE CLASS!

The next topic that {LEO} wants to look at is

ROUNDING UP and DOWN!

Rounding means that you are adjusting numbers so that they become EASIER to work with.

It makes a number simpler...!

... But still close to what it was before.

For instance, I could round a number off to the

nearest ten...

When rounding to the nearest 10, look at the {units} column. If the number in the units column is less than 5, it gets rounded DOWN.

If it is 5 or more, it gets rounded UP.

Look at 27. It is between 20 and 30, but it is nearest to 30.

So 27 could be rounded UP to 30.

2 ¦ 7

The 7 pushes the number UP, so the number is rounded up to 30.

Chop it here.

Now look at {22}. It is also between ((20 and 30)), but this time it is nearer to (20)

So, 22 gets rounded **down** to (20)...!

2 ¦ 2

Chop it here.

The 2 doesn't change the tens column, so the number is rounded down to 20.

Here's some **numbers** I have to sort out.

Round these numbers to the nearest *ten*.

1) 38 ⇨ [ ] 2) 72 ⇨ [ ]

3) 129 ⇨ [ ] 4) 377 ⇨ [ ]

5) 452 ⇨ [ ] 6) 65 ⇨ [ ]

Answers on page 141.

Remember - the 5 moves this one up.

I thought I'd try some of these out on **BOB.**

Sadly, he got them right !

I think he's getting better at **Maths.**

It must be **my** tutoring that's doing it !!

I can also (round) numbers to the nearest 100 in the same way!

2 6 7 rounds up to 3 0 0, because I chop it

after the hundreds column.

4 4 8 rounds down to 4 0 0 for the same reason.

It doesn't matter what is in the units column.

The tens column and the units column change to 0.

I can round numbers to the nearest 1,000 as well.

I must chop the number after the thousands column.

The hundreds, tens and units columns all change to 0.

I thought so! Here comes the homework...!

Round these numbers to the nearest hundred.

1) 6 7 3 [ ]   2) 4 2 9 [ ]

3) 1, 4 4 7 [ ]   4) 2, 3 4 2 [ ]

Round these numbers to the nearest thousand.

5) 3, 9 4 6 [ ]   6) 1, 3 8 8 [ ]

7) 7, 5 0 9 [ ]   8) 5, 4 6 1 [ ]

Answers on page 141.

But... here's a PROBLEM...!

If I'm rounding {397} to the nearest ten,

I {chop} it after the (9) in the tens column.

3 9 | 7   The (7) pushes the hundreds column up.

But... how can I put |10| in the hundreds column?

Well...? I can't!

I have to move the hundreds column {up} one more,

so :397: gets rounded up to :400:!

So, to the nearest |ten|, :97: rounds up to :100,:

and, to the nearest |hundred|, 895 becomes :900.:

:997: gets rounded up over two columns.

It becomes 1000 when rounded to the nearest 10.

I'm confused!

It's not easy. BOB would never understand this!

(I'm not sure I do, either...!)

116

Here's a few ROUNDING PROBLEMS to do...

Round these to the nearest TEN...

1)   519 → [   ]   2) 2399 → [   ]

Round these to the nearest HUNDRED...

3)   693 → [   ]   4) 5695 → [   ]

Round these to the nearest THOUSAND...

5) 7932 → [   ]   6) 18948 → [   ]

In the last {two} the hundreds, tens and units columns all have :0: in them. Answers end → o O O

I'm beginning to understand it a bit better!

DECIMALS can also be rounded UP or DOWN.

I can round numbers to the (nearest) → unit.

I just {chop} them where the (decimal point) is !

2 3 . 4 gets rounded down to (23).

2 3 . 7 gets rounded UP to (24).

This is called {rounding} to the nearest WHOLE NUMBER !

I can also (round) numbers to the nearest tenth.

4 7 . 3 ¦ 8 gets rounded UP to   47.4

4 7 . 3 ¦ 4 gets rounded DOWN to 4 7 . 3

This is called (rounding) to (one decimal place.)

I can also round to two, three or more

decimal places!

Round these numbers to the nearest unit.

1) 7 5 . 7 → [ ]   2) 2 3 8 . 4 → [ ]

3) 8 5 3 . 8 → [ ]   4) 2 6 . 7 2 → [ ]

5) 1 2 . 4 8 → [ ]

6) 3 . 8 2 3 → [ ]

I can just ignore the 2 here.
It doesn't affect the answer.

And the 2 and 3 here.

Now (round) these to the nearest tenth.

7) 3 2 . 6 9 → [ ]   8) 6 . 3 4 7 → [ ]

9) 7 5 . 8 3 → [ ]   10) 0 . 9 6 3 → [ ]

I think I'm getting the hang of these now, but that last one is tricky!

I asked LEO ~ (Why do we do rounding? Where is it useful?)

He says (rounding) is useful in estimating numbers. If I want to get a rough idea of what 48×31 is, I can think of it as 50×30. That makes it easy!

$$\begin{array}{r} 5\,0 \\ \times\ 3\,0 \\ \hline 1,5\,0\,0 \end{array}$$

If the numbers end in zeros, the zeros simply drop down to the answer line!

If I want to estimate what 208×39 is,

I can round those numbers to 200×40

All I do then is multiply 2 x 4 and move all the zeros down to the answer line, so the answer is 8,000!

It's the same if I want to estimate 6.9×5.2

I can round those decimals to 7×5

...which makes it much easier!

I know what's coming! Lots of [ESTIMATING]!

Estimate each of these.

1) 29 x 62   [   ] x [   ] = [   ]

2) 202 x 38   [   ] x [   ] = [   ]

3) 79 x 303   [   ] x [   ] = [   ]

4) 3.9 x 5.1 [   ] x [   ] = [   ]

5) 8.8 x 3.2 [   ] x [   ] = [   ]

6) 497 x 2.9 [   ] x [   ] = [   ]

Estimating also helps with dividing...!

For instance, if you want to estimate [397 ÷ 7.9],

just think of it as [400 ÷ 8], which is (50)!

Here's a few {division} sums that I have to do.

7) 198 ÷ 2.1   [   ] ÷ [   ] = [   ]

8) 597 ÷ 2.9   [   ] ÷ [   ] = [   ]

9) 79 ÷ 3.8   [   ] ÷ [   ] = [   ]

10) 103 ÷ 49   [   ] ÷ [   ] = [   ]

(Answers on page 141.)

HELP! My head is SPINNING...

I'm fed up with anything to do with

ROUNDING...
UP, DOWN or inside out!

I need another maths-free zone!

So you will never see MATHS on this page!

At the moment, I just don't care

how close to the bottom of the class I am!

My cat has got it right...

She knows how to relax

and unwind!

This is Maisie after her tea!

Leave me alone!

I've had another **MATHS TEST** in school.
It covered all the number skills
that we have covered so far [this term] ...
So I knew most of it ... !
I did :quite: well ... (not brilliantly!)
I made a few careless mistakes,
but I was in the { top half } of the class !
Mr Campbell said I have done [well] ! →

And as far as MUM is concerned,
she's pleased that I'm
making good progress !
But she says that LEO THE LION
needs to cover a { lot }
more things with me ...

I ALMOST give up !

Ok! She actually
said Mr Prentice!

I'm not sure she will EVER
be :entirely happy: with my [Maths skills] !

One thing that came up in that **Maths Test**
that I **haven't looked at** yet with Mr P. is...

NEGATIVE NUMBERS.

When we did them in school, I didn't understand them.
It just sounded **weird** at the time... !

Mr P. says that **Negative Numbers** are numbers
that are **lower than zero.**

He gave me a **number line** to explain what he means.

Any number <u>below</u> zero is a **negative** number.

Negative Numbers always have a ⊖ sign in front of them.

Any number <u>above</u> zero is a **positive** number.

Positive numbers are written with <u>no sign</u> or a ⊕ sign.

ZERO isn't positive or negative !

The number line goes on for EVER in both directions.

When I go to the right, the number gets bigger.

When I go to the left, the number gets smaller.

So, -5 is a smaller number than -3 ...

It's bigger by 2 because it is two places to the right on the number line.

I can imagine it as if it is a temperature scale.

| If the temperature is lower than 0° the weather gets colder. It goes into negative degrees. | Freezing point for water is 0 degrees. | If the temperature is higher than 0°, the weather gets warmer. It stays in positive degrees. |

He gave me a TEST. That little ° means degrees.

Rewrite these numbers in order, from smallest to biggest.

4	-2	8	-7	0	-5

Here's the **answers!** (I got them right!)

| -7 | -5 | -2 | 0 | 4 | 8 |

Now I've got a few more to do... (surprise, surprise!)

Rewrite these in order, (smallest to biggest.)

a)

| 9 | -8 | 5 | -1 | -6 | 1 |

b)

| -18 | 21 | 3 | -17 | 2 | -10 |

c)

| -6 | -35 | -23 | -30 | 0 | -24 |

Now Mr P. wants me to look at (Answers on page 142.)

ADDING and Subtracting

{ NEGATIVE NUMBERS. }

He says that I can use a a number line to work out the answer.

If I'm adding, I count right along the line. If I'm subtracting, I count left along the line.

Leo has given me an example to do...!

He asks: if the temperature was (-2°) last night, and then the temperature goes up to (7°) today, by how much has the temperature gone up?

I need a number line to work this one out.

-3 -2 -1 0 1 2 3 4 5 6 7 8 9

That's {nine} places to the right, so the temperature has gone UP by 9 degrees!

Then he told me to look at my fridge freezer ...?!

It said the {temperature} in the fridge is | 2° |
and the {temperature} in the freezer is | -9° |

So he asked what the difference is between them?

-10 -9 -8 -7 -6 -5 -4 -3 -2 -1 0 1 2

That's 12 places to the left, so the freezer is 12 degrees COLDER than the fridge!

Leo's **jokes** are terrible...

After all that work, I'm feeling a bit

NEGATIVE myself...!

I hate negative numbers. I'll stop at nothing to avoid them!

But I wish I knew all that stuff **before** my test!

Mr P. has set me [homework] – **as usual!**

Use this {number line} to answer these questions.

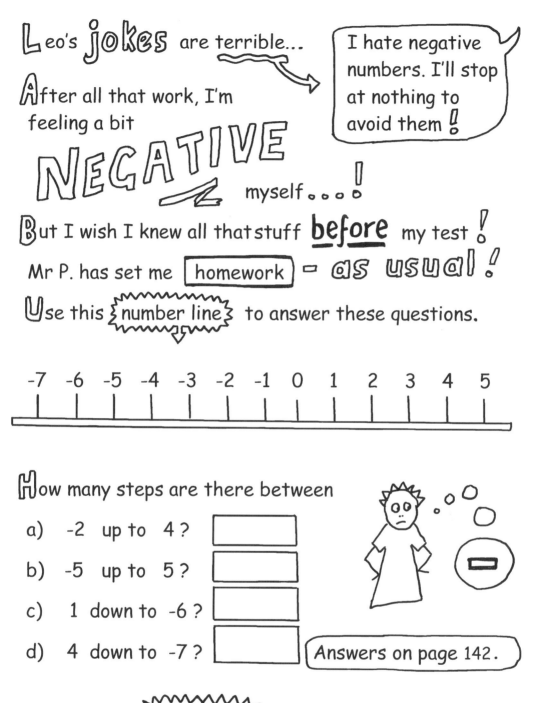

-7 -6 -5 -4 -3 -2 -1 0 1 2 3 4 5

How many steps are there between

a) -2 up to 4 ? [   ]

b) -5 up to 5 ? [   ]

c) 1 down to -6 ? [   ]

d) 4 down to -7 ? [   ]

Answers on page 142.

Using a {number line} is useful, but you'll find that you don't need to use it to find the answer.

Now Mr P. wants me to do the same thing **without** using a ～number line～ !?

He says that if I think about (2 - 7),

it is (7) less than (2) which works out as (-5),

and if I think about (- 3 - 6), it comes to (-9).

I can ﹗even﹗ work out a sum like (2 - 4 + 3).

(2) take away (4) is (-2) and then add (3) = |1|

I'm not sure about all this ...

but I suppose if had (50p.), and then spent (30p.) of it, and then found (20p.) more,

then I'd have (40p.) left.

(50p. - 30p. + 20p. = 40p.)

(I think I'd be lucky to have that much money!)

Here's some for me to do.

a)   3 - 5 = [   ]   b)   4 - 8 = [   ]

c)   5 - 7 + 1 = [   ]   d)   8 - 3 - 7 = [   ]

e)   What is 8 less than 2 ? [   ] | Answers on

f)   What is 7 more than -9 ? [   ] | page 142 .

These are ～difficult!～ I'm starting to HATE maths!

Leo has left me some **more** homework to do ... !
Here's some different **temperatures**
of some cities in the World...

Paris	12°	Moscow	-13°	Rome	18°
London	-2°	Barcelona	16°	Edinburgh	-5°

What is the (difference in temperature) between

a) London and Paris ?

b) Rome and Edinburgh ?

Answers on
page 142.

c) Barcelona and Paris ?

d) Moscow and London ?

e) Which two cities have the
biggest differences in
temperature ?

f) What is the
difference
between them ?

I tried these out on **BOB**...

... but he couldn't work out what to do !
I'm going to have to **explain** to him
how **Negative Numbers** work !

129

Mr P. says that this leads on to looking at

FUNCTION MACHINES!

When I put a number into a { Function machine },

it gives me a number **back out!**

So, if I put (6) in, and then [add 3],

then [multiply it by 4], (36) comes out.

I can show it this way ⇒

(6) ⇨ [+ 3] ⇨ [x 4] ⇨ (36)

Now here's some that I have to do...

a) 7 ⇨ [x 3] ⇨ [+ 5] ⇨ [   ]

b) 12 ⇨ [- 4] ⇨ [+ 6] ⇨ [   ]

c) 8 ⇨ [- 3] ⇨ [x 8] ⇨ [   ]

Now I have to find answers to these, using this set

of { function boxes. } ⇨ [÷3]   [+ 2]   [x 7]

d) 6 ⇨ [   ] ⇨ [   ] ⇨ [   ]

e) 15 ⇨ [   ] ⇨ [   ] ⇨ [   ]

f) 3 ⇨ [   ] ⇨ [   ] ⇨ [   ]

(They're not <u>too</u> bad !)   (Answers on page 142. ⇨)

130

The **tricky** bit is when I'm told what comes **out** of the {machine} and then I have to find what was **put in !?**

| These | are very *important things* I **need** to know!

- The opposite of ⊕ is ⊖ , and
- the opposite of ⊗ is ⊘ !

In a { function machine, } if I'm going **backwards,** I have to do the 'OPPOSITE' of what the machine says...

The function box here says ⟹ | × 4 | | +3 |

So if (23) comes **OUT** of the *function machine,* then (23) | -3 | | ÷4 | , so (5) went **in !**

I have to work out what number went {in} to these, in order to work out what came {out.}

a) [ ] ← | × 2 | ← | + 5 | ← | 17 |

b) [ ] ← | ÷ 3 | ← | - 7 | ← | 11 |

c) [ ] ← | - 8 | ← | × 4 | ← | 16 |

d) [ ] ← | - 2 | ← | ÷ 7 | ← | 4 |

(Much more difficult!) (Answers on page 142.)

MAISIE is disgusted with all this Maths! ⬇

She hates my tutor almost as much as she hates BOB!

But, sadly, MUM thinks Mr P. is great!

As far as I'm concerned, LEO isn't {too bad!} He has helped me

to improve my Maths, and at least I'm NOT Bottom Of The Class any more!

Thankfully, it's nearly the END OF TERM, which means that...

a) I get two week's holiday,

and b) I only have one more session with Mr P.

and then I get a break for a while!

I thought that {Mr P} would give me an easy time!
Instead, I've got loads of hard work to do...

He says this next test will check whether I've been paying attention to him this term!
It's all about completing SEQUENCES.

I have to work out the missing numbers in these.
Some are EASY. Some are DIFFICULT!

a) 25   29   33   37   ☐

b) 18   14   10   6   ☐

c) 7   14   ☐   28   35

d) 3   6   12   24   ☐

e) 6.7   ☐   6.1   5.8   5.5

f) 200   100   50   ☐   ☐

g) 25   36   49   64   ☐

h) 84   ☐   108   120   132

i) 1   8   27   ☐   125

j) 20   14   8   2   ☐

k) -11   -8   -5   -2   ☐

l) 2   3   5   7   11   ☐   ☐

They were so°°o difficult! The answers to all those sequences are on page 143. Don't cheat!

I got 8 out of 12, so that's not too bad!

The last one was the worst...

LEO was RIGHT...!

I had to know everything I've looked at this term.

I suppose overall I've made good progress,

and at least I'm popular with Mr Campbell now!

I don't struggle with my maths as much,

so there are a few things to show

for all that hard work.

Overall, I think Maisie has it right.

She just takes life easy!

No WORRIES! No STRESS!

And the reason for that is...

MY CAT HATES MATHS!

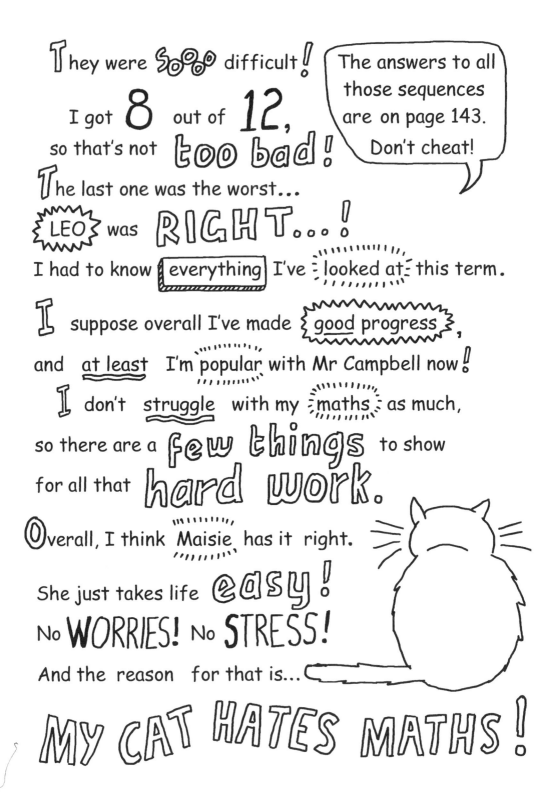

135

Answers...

19

1. 12,016   2. 15,100   3. 35,015   4. 9,009

5.   5 is in the hundreds column = 500

6.   4 is in the tens of thousands column.

7.   9 is in the units column = 9

20

1)   39, 44, 45, 50, 71, 72

2)   69, 78, 463, 984, 4, 12,032

21

1)   87,521   2)   12,578

3)   Three hundred and six.

4)   Four thousand and twelve.

5)   Two hundred and six thousand and fifty.

22

1)   157   2)   1,730   3)   275

27

248, 135, 127, 2,138, 7,428, 566

First one [3] Second one [3] Third one [5]

[4]   [1] [8]   [2]

[6]

38

Missing multiples of 3 = 3, 9, 12

Missing multiples of 7 = 14, 21, 28

Missing multiples of 8 = 8, 24, 40

41

108, 336, 266, 730, 2,184, 1,077, 3,843, 1,872, 1,211

More Answers...

43   1,215, 2,142, 1,035, 7,072, 10,621, 11,808

47   1) 290   2) 750   3) 1,620   4) 4,730
      5) 67   6) 85

48   1) 370 2) 790 3) 4,500 4) 6,100
      5) 56,000 6) 9,700 7) 2,350 8) 45,700

52   a) 153   b) 165   c) 124   d) 296
      e) 123   f) 125   g) 239   h) 119

54   1) 6.7   2) 1.8   3) 45.8   4) 30.4
      5) 12.3 6) 0.2

55   1) 6.52 2) 0.47 3) 30.68 4) 12.943
      5) 0.572 6) 0.301

57   90,000   200,000   14,000   3   2   20

63   a) 2.4   b) 16.5   c) 6.5   d) 13.5
      e) 11.5   f) 15.2   g) 17.75 h) 6.25

65   1) 427.53   2) 5.46   3) 8.66

69   1) 0.33,   3.3,   33,   330
      2) 0.8,   8,   80,   800
      3) 0.09,   0.5,   7,   48
      4) 0.56,   0.8,   6.5,   26

70   a) 8.7 b) 9.3 1) 2.5 2) 8.4 3) 24.5

Even More Answers...

71   1) 5.5   2) 3.7   3) 10.3   4) 16.3   5) 4.5

76   1) $\dfrac{3}{5}$ 2) $\dfrac{5}{8}$ 3) $\dfrac{1}{6}$ 4) $\dfrac{3}{4}$

78    $\dfrac{2}{8} = \dfrac{1}{4}$ $\dfrac{6}{12} = \dfrac{1}{2}$ $\dfrac{9}{12} = \dfrac{3}{4}$

     $\dfrac{10}{20} = \dfrac{1}{2}$ $\dfrac{12}{15} = \dfrac{4}{5}$ $\dfrac{6}{20} = \dfrac{3}{10}$

82   1) $\dfrac{4}{6}$ $\dfrac{5}{6}$ $\dfrac{3}{6}$ → $\dfrac{5}{6}$ 2) $\dfrac{6}{8}$ $\dfrac{5}{8}$ $\dfrac{4}{8}$ → $\dfrac{3}{4}$

     3) $\dfrac{6}{10}$ $\dfrac{5}{10}$ $\dfrac{7}{10}$ → $\dfrac{7}{10}$ 4) $\dfrac{2}{12}$ $\dfrac{3}{12}$ $\dfrac{4}{12}$ → $\dfrac{1}{3}$

     5) $\dfrac{14}{16}$ $\dfrac{12}{16}$ $\dfrac{13}{16}$ → $\dfrac{7}{8}$

83   1) 15   2) 10   3) 4   4) 32   5) 28

85   1) $\dfrac{4}{12} = \dfrac{2}{6} = \dfrac{8}{24} = \dfrac{1}{3}$ 2) $\dfrac{3}{5} = \dfrac{9}{15} = \dfrac{18}{30} = \dfrac{6}{10}$

     3) $\dfrac{2}{8} = \dfrac{10}{40} = \dfrac{5}{20} = \dfrac{1}{4}$

Yet More Answers!

Page	Answers

90   1) a) 20% b) 75% c) 33% d) 90%

         2) a) 40% b) 66 or 67% c) 33%

            d) 40% e) 25%

91)   20% 2) 80% 3) 75% 4) 60%

        5) 90% 6) 40%

92   1) 15 2) 72 3) 48 4) 9   5) 21

99     $21 = 1 \times 21, 3 \times 7$

        $24 = 1 \times 24, 2 \times 12, 3 \times 8, 4 \times 6$

        $28 = 1 \times 28, 2 \times 14, 4 \times 7$

        $32 = 1 \times 32, 2 \times 16, 4 \times 8$

        $35 = 1 \times 35, 5 \times 7$

102)   31 and 37 are the prime numbers.

         2) 41, 43, 47 and 53 are all prime numbers.

103   3) a) 17   b) 29   c) 47

       4) a) 11   b) 23

       5) a) 5 and 7   b) 61 and 67

110   Five square numbers: 9, 36, 49, 64 and 81.

        Four cube numbers: 8, 27, 64 and 125.

And More Answers...

111   1) 5^2 = 25   2) 6^2 = 36   3) 8^2 = 64
         4) 2^3 = 8   5) 4^3 = 64   6) 5^3 = 125
         7) 6^3 = 216
         8)   3 + 6 = 9,   5 + 11 = 16,
             7 + 18 = 25,   8 + 28 = 36

112   1) 5   2) 7   3) 6   4) 9

114   1) 40   2) 70   3) 130   4) 380
         5) 450   6) 70

115   1) 700   2) 400   3) 1,400   4) 2,300
         5) 4,000   6) 1,000   7) 8,000   8) 5,000

117   1) 520   2) 2,400   3) 700   4) 5,700
         5) 8,000   6) 19,000

118   1) 76   2) 238   3) 854   4) 27   5) 12
         6) 4   7) 32.7   8) 6.3   9) 75.8   10) 1

120   1) 30 x 60 = 1,800   2) 200 x 40 = 8,000
         3) 80 x 300 = 24,000   4) 4 x 5 = 20
         5) 9 x 3 = 27   6) 500 x 3 = 1,500
         7) 200 ÷ 2 = 100   8) 600 ÷ 3 = 200
         9) 80 ÷ 4 = 20   10) 100 ÷ 50 = 2

How Many More Answers?

125   a)   -8, -6, -1, 1, 5, 9
         b)   -18, -17, -10, 2, 3, 21
         c)   -35, -30, -24, -23, -6, 0

127   a)   6   b)   10   c)   7   d)   11

128   a) -2   b)   -4   c) -1   d)   -2   e) -6   f) -2

129   a) $14°$ b) $23°$ c) $4°$ d) $11°$
       e) Moscow and Rome.
          There's $31°$ between them.

130   a)   26   b)   14   c)   40
         d)   6→2→4→28   e) 15→5→7→49
         f)   3→1→3→21

131   a)   6   b)   6   c)   12   d)   30

Far too much work...!

...And here's the **answers** to that

Sequences on page { 133 }! Test

a) 41   The numbers are going up by 4 each time.

b) 2   The numbers are going down by 4 each time.

c) 21   It's the seven times table.

d) 48   The numbers are doubling each time.

e) 6.4   Each number is a going down by 0.3

f) 25, then 12.5 or $12\frac{1}{2}$. The numbers are halving.

g) 81   These are all square numbers in ascending order.

h) 96   This is the twelve times table.

i) 64   This is a list of the cube numbers in ascending order.

j) -4   The numbers are going down by 6 each time.

k) 1   The numbers are going up by 3 each time.

l) 13, 17   This is a list of prime numbers in ascending order! If you got these ones, you're doing well

Printed in Great Britain
by Amazon